FALLING IN LOVE
WITH GOD

Falling in Love with God

A Personal Message to Today's Young People from St. Francis de Sales

By Michel Tournade, OSFS

An Adaptation of the Introduction to the Devout Life

DeSales Resource Center
Stella Niagara, NY
2015

Title of the French original:
UN MONDE À AIMER
Une adaptation de L'Introduction a la View Devote
de saint Francois de Sales
Michel Tournade
Deuxieme Edition
collection Spiritualite
nouvelle cite
Le Vieil Annecy

English Translation by Janet Gowey

Cover Art by Thomas Ribits, OSFS

Published by DeSales Resource Center
Stella Niagara, NY 14144
1-800-782-2270

Library of Congress Control Number: 2015956878
ISBN 978-0-9713199-3-6

To order: 1-800-782-2270
www.EmbracedbyGod.org

CONTENTS

Publisher's Preface

This volume by Michel Tournade, an Oblate of St. Francis de Sales of the French Province, was originally written and copyrighted in French in 1998. It has had a great deal of success in French and we were very interested in getting it into English.

Janet Gowey was so kind and generous as to volunteer to offer us the first English script. In order to contemporize the text for an American young audience, we asked Oblate Thomas Ribits of the American Provinces to read it together with young college-aged adults and offer feedback and suggestions for the final editing. A very special thanks to Tylor Vaillaincourt, Zach Smith, and Jordon Vokes who spent much time reviewing and writing down notes. Final editing was the responsibility of DeSales Resources and Ministries, Inc.

We not only hope that this work is authentic to what Michel Tournade adapted from St. Francis de Sales, but also very helpful in the spiritual life of our young people.

Notice to the Reader
from MICHEL TOURNADE

I must ask St. Francis de Sales' pardon, because this book, Un Monde a Aimer, is a kind of betrayal.

While defending a thesis for my doctorate at the University of Metz, I experienced, like so many before me, great pleasure while studying the beautiful language of the sixteenth and seventeenth centuries in which the Bishop of Geneva wrote in such a personal way, referring to those reading as *"Philothea"* and *"Theotimus."*

I was convinced that, like climbing a mountain to view creation in a new way, an attempt to bring a good Salesian book into a Twenty-first Century view would be worthwhile.

I also regretted seeing this spiritual treasure of our church being set aside simply because of an antiquated literary style. Francis was a dynamic, enterprising bishop who wrote for his time, in language and style that was popular and understood in that moment, enabling him to share with others the wonderful spiritual experience he had come to know. The first title of his work was Introduction to the Devout Life.

This is an *"adaptation."* Is it wrong to make the view from the mountaintop more accessible? If we imagine that Bishop De Sales is prepping his diocese for an important celebration, he would speak simply and with familiarity to "*Philothea*", who may be a college student, an artist, a nurse, or computer technician or perhaps to "*Theotimus*"—the young med student, the baseball player—in short—to anyone preparing for any career in life.

This adaptation seeks to retain the essence and ideas of De Sales who loved creation, nature so deeply, and who was so intimately engaged in loving this world. As Bullet trains and instantaneous communication through the Internet have replaced older and slower forms of transportation and communication, updated examples reflect the reality of our own time.

In this book you are invited to discover and explore the spiritual foundation that Francis De Sales presents, and to respond to the immense love that God has for you.

In the future, my hope is that you may find a reason to discover the works of Saint Francis in their original form

Fr. Michel Tournade
Oblate of St. Francis de Sales

The Salesian Path

Have you ever looked intently at the work of artists who specialize in floral compositions? The paintings are amazing. They always seem to be fresh and new, yet they always remain the same flowers. But each time we see them it is our own impression that is different and changing! The Holy Spirit works the same way with us and in us. Let me explain. The Gospel—the good news of Jesus Christ—that has been given to us is unique. It was revealed to us in a different culture and time long ago, yet it is the same but always fresh and new. The way of living out its principles and adapting it to lived situations in today's world make it extraordinarily pliable and varied, fitted to the talent and gifts of each individual person. It is not a museum piece and so it is important to live it in the reality of our day and age.

You may think, even be convinced that a real relationship with God is not for you; that it is reserved for "holy" people like monks and nuns...and you certainly don't have a great desire to "leave or flee the world" and live behind a wall. That's OK. But it is my hope in this work to speak with you in very simple terms about a realistic way of living your faith as a young Christian immersed in the busyness of all that makes up your daily life. You don't have to wait until you are older, or for retirement, or for a possible religious vocation to experience this. You can live this experience of faith here and now. There is an old story about oysters grown for pearls...It seems that they live in the middle of the ocean, yet the pearls they produce never become corroded by the ocean's salty water. It's sort of the same way for us. Don't think that it's by fleeing the reality of your situation that you will find God. You can protect that valuable pearl which is your faith and live in the middle of a society and world that are not very easy to live in.

Simply put, it's not too practical to grow in your spiritual and interior life all by yourself. It's helpful to have someone or something to guide you along the way. I want to offer myself for that purpose and to share with you a little of my own experiences. I've done this for others who have given me the opportunity to show them this path. I hope this will help you. I've tried to keep it short, since I don't have too much time to myself to write to you...and probably because you don't have too much time to read long letters either! I'll try to speak to you as clearly as possible.

I also have a word for anyone who may have a chance to join you in your reflections. I also wish them happiness—the joy that comes from giving and helping someone to grow and experience what life offers more deeply.

In any case, that's the joy I experienced in finding my way down the road that others first showed me. Please understand that if I allow myself to give you spiritual advice, it is certainly not because I'm perfect! I doubt that you would want advice from a perfect person anyway! I am just like you; I just want to stumble less and less and to develop my virtues as best as possible.

As we begin I have one last thought...do you like ancient history? Probably not, I imagine, and that's OK. There's a story that Alexander the Great commissioned a famous painter of his time with the job of painting the portrait of an attractive young lady he desired. In order to complete the work, the artist had to study and reflect upon his model for a long time. In the process, over time, the artist fell in love with her. He fell so deeply in love with her that Alexander noticed, and with compassion changed his own intention and allowed the artist to marry her. It's a beautiful story that speaks to me from my own experience. As a result of painting the portrait of my encounter with the Lord for others, I am falling more and more in love every day with this God whom I discover more and more each day.

I wish you a good spiritual journey with Him and every blessing too!

At Annecy
Feast of Saint Mary Magdalen, 1609

+Francis De Sales

PART ONE

CHAPTER 1

To begin well

If you want to develop your interior life, it's really a question of not making a mistake as you begin your journey. As an example, if you develop bad habits when learning a sport or any other activity, these habits can end up being hard to get rid of later on—can't they. It's the same way when you are learning to deepen your interior life. There are bad habits as well that are good to avoid.

Sometimes you will hear some people say that there is a certain prayer style, or a popular new technique to bring about spiritual experiences and that that is a good way to proceed. In a way these things can seduce us into thinking that this is the only way to go about deepening our spiritual life. This can be likened to a painter who only paints the woman he loves in all his works, believing she is the only subject worthy of interest. You have probably observed in your life, and found it amusing, that some teachers would be better off if they kept quiet because all they make is a lot of noise! I know some people who make large donations to charity, yet they don't pardon the smallest fault of their neighbor. Others would never think of missing Mass, yet they kill their neighbor with malicious gossip. Look out! These types turn people off to a positive spiritual experience. Seek a teacher who is not self-centered and lives what they teach by good and balanced example.

The first and most important realization necessary in order to be united to God is to know that God unconditionally loves you. Because you are so deeply loved, this awareness will help you to grow and transform you completely. As you realize you have received so much from God, you will begin to serve others more genuinely. This love, the giving of self in service brings us into solidarity with others and as it becomes more integrated in us, draws us to be compassionately united to, with and in God.

Every bird has wings. Ostriches hardly ever use them. If you have ever seen a chicken fly, you know that it is not a pretty sight. Eagles, hawks and swallows are graceful and magnificent in flight. The same can be true of people in the spiritual life. Some people never understand that having an interior life can cause them to fly. Others are so insecure and worried about what others think of them that they don't know whether or not they are going down a path chosen for them by God. Yet others come to appreciate their interior life that pushes them like second nature to love others and to serve them. You can understand by now that those in this last category are genuinely united to God, not only by their works, but also in action.

You might be thinking that serving others will mean a life filled with unlimited duties and obligations, and that to follow the commandment to love will create so many demands that it is going to ruin your life by tying you down. If that's the way you see things, you may be blinding yourself and smothering any motivation to even try serving others. I can tell you this, serving others not only brings joy to them, but also makes us deeply happy ourselves!

If your friends invite you for a hike, skiing, cycling or even a walk after you've had a long illness or an operation, any effort on your part is going to seem really hard and painful. But once you heal and your energy returns, you experience great pleasure in hiking that trail, swooshing down that mountain, rounding the turns or just walking through the neighborhood with your friends and your renewed energy. It's the same thing in following the path of directions and commandments that God puts in front of you. You will see that action, service, prayer and contemplation (deep prayer and reflection) are inseparable just like a flame is to fire. It is to such a lively, energetic, glowing and sparkling life that your Creator invites you!

CHAPTER 2

To be united with God: yes, but how?

If you open a Bible, you'll see that often people are afraid of life and the future without having any serious reason for fear. This certainly was the case for the people of Israel as they journeyed in the desert. I'll admit that the description of the Promised Land given by the first scouts sent there was pretty horrifying. They reported that the climate was unhealthy and the land inhabited by brutal giants. The reality was something completely different and as you can imagine, this turned into a very real surprise for them!

All around you, many people talk about religion in the same way those first scouts portrayed the Promised Land. These people would have us believe that the Christian life is a somewhat neurotic, bi-polar, and a completely unrealistic lifestyle. Luckily, in the biblical text, Joshua saw past the gloom and has a completely different idea. Meeting his God, he dared to lead the people of God to this infamous *"Promised Land!"* Inspired by the Spirit and getting past the gloom, you too will see that meeting your God will lead you to find happiness!

We have to have the courage to take the plunge. You know that making the choice to put your faith into practice means sharing, placing yourself in the service of those who are suffering, dealing with and overcoming your impulsive nature, understanding and setting limits on your desires, and also, not giving in or letting your sensual appetites rule and run your life.

Often all of this makes us think of repression and renunciation. You say to yourself: *"I've got to deprive myself of anything that gives me pleasure or happiness; I'll have to avoid showing affection; I'll always have to restrain myself."* You imagine or see lots of negatives that might seem heroic perhaps, but they don't inspire your enthusiasm at all.

You're forgetting, and not seeing then in this analysis, one very important essential dimension: that of <u>true</u> happiness. To choose the Christian life is to choose authentic pleasure and true happiness.

When bees gather nectar, they actually find a very bitter substance. However, they are able to transform it into honey. Likewise, if you don't learn to choose and actually prefer the Christian life, giving up things and taming your desires will undeniably seem utterly bitter to you. *"Preferring God,"* however, will gradually and naturally transform your efforts into the pleasure you seek and you will experience true happiness in doing so. A biblical saying describes it this way: *"a fire in winter and roses in summer..."*

Read the story of Jacob's dream in the Book of Genesis 28:10-17. In it he saw a ladder that joined heaven with earth. A constant coming and going, ascending and descending energized the ladder. I interpret that dream as a good description of the choice you are invited to make. You are called constantly to bend over and reach out to others, to be loving and attentive to them. At the same time you are invited to climb—to discover your God more and more in your personal history and in the incidences and coincidences that occur each day of your life.

In his dream, Jacob saw some creatures that he called "*angels*" going up and down the ladder. These creatures were human in form. This gave them a more solid and lively appearance. They also had beautiful faces as well. This picture gives us a pretty good idea of what the Christian life can be. It's dynamic and holds nothing that is sad, shabby or ugly in store for us!

CHAPTER 3

You can live in union with God in the midst of any activity

When we observe nature, and more specifically ours or a neighbor's garden we can see great variety among the plants. Each, even among the same species, is different. It grows at its own pace and produces its fruit at its own pace and in its own time. It's the same with human beings—each of us is individual and unique. We are the plants within the garden of the God's church. God the gardener, wants nothing more than that we grow, develop and produce according to our potential.

Each person obviously, the executive, the artist, the student and the teacher will need to cultivate and nourish their Christian life in the garden where they find themselves planted. Think of this—What kind of bishop would spend his life dreaming of isolation and life lived in a desert hut or a remote monastery. Parents who gave away everything to be poor like begging monks would be acting irresponsibly toward their children. Office employees who wanted to spend eight hours a day in prayer in a church like a monk or large portions of their workday in a soup kitchen would be quickly fired!

Do you think I'm exaggerating? Not entirely, unfortunately, I know some people who always want to live in another way rather than in the way they are called! That's due, not to a desire to live out their faith, but to their wistful thinking, degrees of jealously and greed, poor judgment and an unrealistic *"what if?"*

It's my conviction and belief that union with God will not interfere in any way with the way you live. Your studies, hobbies, work, and the sports you play—you don't have to give any of them up! If you are honest, you will live every aspect of your life most intensely with lots of energy.

I like bees so I'm going to use them for another example. Bees extract their honey from flowers without causing any damage to them. Likewise, living your life in union with God does something even better...because like the bee you will extract the honey of life from your relationship with God and what you are doing without hurting the flower of your activities.

It's a serious mistake to think that soldiers, business people, politicians and families cannot live closely united to God. It's true that a purely contemplative life—such as lived by monks and nuns in a monastery—can't be lived while practicing those professions. But there are plenty of other opportunities to live a God-centered life. Many seekers have gone before us; Abraham, Isaac, Jacob, David, Ruth, Ester, David and Job are great examples.

There are people in our own day and age that we can look up to in the same way.

Perhaps you can think of some contemporary examples, not just a Mother Teresa or Martin Luther King, Jr., but how about some exceptional people you have known in your own life.

All of them are unique with their gifts, talents, jobs, their lived adventures and in the choices they make. Some people who really struggled to live God-centered lives in solitude as monks or nuns, have succeeded in living the Christian life well in regular everyday society which isn't always supportive.

Whoever we are, wherever we are, we can and are able to desire and seek union with our God, live compassionately in the example of the Lord, and walk the path that leads to being fully human that is the essence of what it means to be holy!

CHAPTER 4

Choosing a good guide

Another book in the Bible also speaks about Love. It's the Book of Tobit. [In some Bibles you'll only find Tobit in a section called the Apocrypha.] The young hero is someone who gradually understands how he can overcome many obstacles with love. This young man leaves on a trip to a foreign country that doesn't have a very good reputation. In the beginning, he's a little frightened, and he's not sure how he's going to get there. His Dad suggests that it might be good to find a good guide, like someone does when they go hiking to a remote area or climb a mountain.

It's sort of the same idea if you want to explore the road that leads to union with God. I suggest that it's good for you to choose an experienced guide to lead you. This really is important advice that I'm giving you. Many Christians who are admired and looked up to in our time have chosen good and solid spiritual companions for the journey.

During your life you've probably had the experience of different relationships that made or even forced you to look seriously into the depth of your heart. Many times the

Bible speaks of this kind of friendship as wonderful—it makes both the guide and the follower grow together. The holy book speaks about it in a marvelous way: *"The faithful friend is a sure help. The one who has found one has found a treasure. The faithful friend is medicine for life and eternity. Those who seek the Presence of God experience this."*

How do we go about finding such a friend? Let's look at the words I just gave you. It speaks of *"those who seek the Presence of God,"* in other words, those who sincerely wish to make progress in their interior and spiritual life. You begin by asking God in all humility and in your prayer to bring a friendly guide into your life to join and guide you down the path of spiritual discovery. Believe me! That is a prayer that God hears particularly well!

You are going to need a lot of humility, and confidence will also be necessary in order for you to really be transparent and share yourself with your guide. The more honestly and openly you express yourself, the deeper this spiritual journey will be. Trust—great trust must be the order of the day between you.

Sometimes it necessarily takes a lot of effort to find someone you can be completely at ease with—and you don't have to be in a hurry. Your spiritual guide must have a friendly open character, personal experience, and self-confidence. When you find this special person, I wish you every grace and blessing on your spiritual journey together!

CHAPTER 5

There are things in you to change

Without meaning to flatter you, I'm sure you are filled with lots of ambition for many things. Ambition can be like weeds in early spring. They can crop up anywhere on a lawn or in a garden and grow in any direction sometimes taking over. Something similar can happen to us— we each have tendencies that are less than shining. We have to look at this reality and take the bull by the horns and sort out the positives and negatives that make us tick. St. Paul encouraged the people of his day to become like *"brand new."* I'm going to challenge you to do the same. I'm going to offer spiritual vitamins and supplements that will strengthen you and help you build a muscular sanctity as strong as a steel framework in your interior.

Sometimes—as it was for St. Paul, the encounter with God is lightening-fast and life is totally changed— definitely transformed in the matter of seconds. We call this *"conversion."* Let's not daydream too much. Cases like Paul's are very rare. You're not likely to have a *"wow"* experience like his! Realistically you will see a slower change in yourself. This won't be easy but it won't be ordinary either.

Think about this. If you ever get up really early in the morning to go walking or biking, you have the opportunity to be part of the miraculous moment when daylight begins to overcome the dark of night...this does not happen suddenly. It happens in small increments—moment by moment. This is really true for summer mornings. It's like that in your spiritual life.

You can also look at it this way. Healing happens in the same way. Illness of the body, mind, or heart arrives pretty fast, like a jet, or a speeding racecar, but many times healing takes place slowly like a lumbering tortoise! And we become impatient.

So this is my advice. Be courageous and patient with yourself. It's sad to see people who take lots of effort to deal with and correct their faults and failings and who become quickly discouraged when they fall into the same habits over and over again. Sometimes they become so discouraged that they abandon everything they have done and end up not liking or even hating themselves. There are also others who convince themselves that they've already overcome their faults and reached virtue after only a day of effort. That's like being a baby bird that starts to fly—with undeveloped wings!

Seeking to improve yourself will last your lifetime, so don't spend a lot of energy in useless worry about your faults. Simply seek to understand them and overcome them. Don't think you'll be able to do this in a week or even by year's end! When God asks you to become *"perfect,"* he really means become *"compassionate,"* and that means being compassionate to yourself to begin with. He knows that *"perfection/compassion"* consists not in covering up or ignoring all your faults, but in accepting them and dealing with them in a positive way. <u>You have to begin by recognizing them.</u>

You will see that it's not a bad thing for you to have some faults. They keep you modest and humble. Those who are too perfect are sometimes out of touch and really boring. Your faults are part of you—so recognize them and don't let them overwhelm you, and more importantly don't let them demoralize you. King David offers us an example when he prays asking God to remove his cowardliness and discouragement. This is a pretty good request! So I offer this advice: be energetic about dealing with your faults, but I forbid you to be discouraged by who you are! Forge ahead—to deal honestly with your reality is to already win!

CHAPTER 6

Begin by attacking what is the most serious

We have a wonderful way to profit by getting to know ourselves in the Sacrament of Reconciliation. We often do not bother with it and take it for granted. It is a magnificent sacrament that if approached with a positive attitude will grow on us. Try it—you will come to like it. It requires that we be honest with ourselves. It can allow you to analyze situations and reread the whole of your life. Sometimes it is said that it's easy enough to go to confession, but if it's only to repeat the same faults again right afterward, then it's hardly worth the trouble. This is probably true for those who confess in a routine manner without giving what they confess much thought beyond listing it.

By bringing up this sacrament, I am speaking here about really <u>working</u> on yourself...in order <u>to know yourself better</u>. Self-knowledge will free you from whatever imprisons you and makes you unhappy. It will also help you know once again how much God unconditionally loves you just as you are. Believe me, in this sacrament you will find healing, serenity, peace and a confidence that can only come with self knowledge rooted in God. This will allow you to really make progress.

But it's hard to just go on talking to you about it; you'll really have to step up to the plate and have a try at it. Can you do this? Can you make a resolution to celebrate and experience this sacrament? Can you experience it soon as a new beginning?

CHAPTER 7

Correct in yourself this mysterious pleasure we can take in doing wrong

When the Israelites left slavery in Egypt and journeyed toward the Promised Land, they did not leave their faults, failings, wants and needs behind! Some behaved and spoke hatefully toward Moses. Why? They remembered only the few good things of their life in Egypt; especially some simple little dishes that in their memory grew more delicious and tasty the longer their journey became. This memory clashed directly with the frugality of gathered food and repeated menu day after day that marked life in the desert.

It's pretty much the same when you come to the Sacrament of Reconciliation. You leave the place that imprisoned your interior in the slavery of egotism and selfishness. But often times you have to admit that deep down inside you might feel a certain longing in leaving that egotism and selfishness behind. In reality, sometimes you'll still look back and desire all those things that you would still like to root out and like to change in yourself.

There's a doctor I know who imposes strict diets on some of his patients. Since he is authoritative and demanding, he terrifies his patients who fear they may be in danger of dying if they don't obey him. The poor people become obsessed by *"doctor's orders"* and they often think lustfully of all their favorite unhealthy dishes that they'll never be able to have again because of the necessary limitations a new healthy diet imposes on them.

And again, there are certain people I know who would like to become filled with virtue this way: follow God, certainly, but while keeping a little tidbit of all they believe is now forbidden to them resting on their taste buds! They think that those who give themselves over to their vices—vices that they themselves want to abandon—are in the end really lucky and maybe even happy. I can assure you that by having that particular attitude they will quickly tire of trying to be virtuous!

I'm also thinking of the example of a certain young man who really wanted to get even for a dirty trick someone once played on him. He realized that this wasn't the Gospel way—that it wasn't what Jesus would do. He was clearly conscious of the fact that he shouldn't act with revenge. But not long afterward, while meeting with some friends, I saw him get upset all over again. He took great pleasure in explaining just how he could make his nemesis pay for the nastiness he experienced. He ended up even bitterly regretting that the gospel *"so stupidly"* required him to be merciful. He told himself that the satisfaction of revenge would really give him great happiness. This young man wanted to break free of his unchristian attitude, on the one hand, but he still held tightly to the tidbit of his old behavior, with the other hand. In reality he resembled those Israelites in the desert who were dreaming about the "*wonderful*" food they left behind in Egypt.

So I hope you understand that wanting to give up your faults, your failings—in short—your sin—also means that you'll have to redirect and refocus your pleasure. As a result, there are bound to be numerous failures, and you'll constantly ask yourself if you are right to really want to live this Christian life. This challenge can seem sort of constricting.

Lastly, I have to be direct and it's not easy to say this. We have to look at apathy. I know some people who are apathetic. False perfection is often the cause—as long as it's easy everything is OK but when things get tough, it's easier to check out. Apathy is a spiritual illness. The person is listless, has no energy and doesn't want to do anything. This is very hard to cure. They just don't care! They're not hungry, don't sleep well, and don't have fun. They just shuffle and push through life with no direction or parameters. There is no growth—no progress—no generosity—no satisfaction—and no reward. Please, O please, guard yourself diligently against becoming apathetic. If you live your Christian life in that way, you'll get sick of it quickly and turn off. And in doing so you'll end up turning off others on becoming Christians too!

CHAPTER 8

How should you change?

In order to get beyond the satisfaction that your faults brought you in the past, I advise you to act decisively and radically: if you come to a realization of regret and feel genuine sorrow for your actions in a powerful and lively new way—we call this contrition—you'll be able to tear yourself away from the attractions and influences that sin produce.

For instance, if you dislike someone, or are bitter toward that person, you may avoid having any interaction with him or her. If this dislike is really strong, bordering on hate, not only will you not be able to bear his/her presence, but you'll also not wish any interaction with his/her friends as well. Even seeing a picture, or coming across something that belongs to that person will cause a reaction.

The same thing happens when you come to detest your own bad conduct; you'll react with the desire never to return to it. If you detest the destructive pleasure and emptiness it brought you just as much, you'll manage more easily not to get into the same rut again. Jesus gives a beautiful and compassionate example of pardon in his relationship with St. Mary Magdalene. That young woman was never again tempted by the degrading, addictive and unhealthy pleasures of her former life.

In order to reach this new outlook and attitude, prayer can be a real support and become a solid foundation. I suggest that you dedicate and set aside fifteen minutes a day for God. If you can do this in the morning, that would be great, because then your whole day will be influenced by this early encounter with your Creator. In addition, I'm going to offer several themes and ideas—let's call them *"meditations"*—they will help you to enter into this personal encounter with your God.

CHAPTER 9

Now here's a little guide for your "conversation" with God— this first meditation is on creation

You have to prepare for this encounter with God like you'd prepare for getting together with friends.

1. I invite you to place yourself in the Presence of God by becoming aware that God is always with you. You can begin by praising and thanking God for life.
2. Ask the Holy Spirit and our Blessed Mother Mary to be your companions with you in your prayer. (It makes it easier—you won't be alone!)

Here are some points that may help you if you reflect upon them.

1. Imagine something totally amazing. Hundreds of years ago you did not exist! You did not exist one year before your birthday! NOW YOU DO! And yet, the awesome work of creation already existed for thousands and thousands of years before your own story even began.
2. God brought you forth from this non-existence, desired that you have life, and gave you your own unique place

in the universe. God wanted you to begin the sacred story that is all your own!

3. Become totally aware of what God has given you. You are made in God's image and you are eternal; yes, made capable of living eternally and united to your creator!

Once you have prayed—let's use "meditated"—on this, I suggest that you look at the following points:

1. Realize how very small you are before God. The Psalm says *"O Lord, I am nothing before you; how can you even gaze upon me?"* (Ps 39:5, 8:4)

2. Thank God for who and what you are. Thank God also for all that you have been given.

3. While you feel this way I ask you to become aware of the fact that you have sometimes strayed from what God has been asking of you—from the reason for which you were given your life.

4. Tell yourself that you are *"the work of God's Hands."* If God has given much to you, God also expects much from you!

5. This part can be tricky—you have to ask yourself this question honestly and answer truthfully! Will you keep the talents you've received all to yourself? Will you hoard them or share them? Think in what way you could share them and turn them into a real response of love and service for this God who unconditionally loves you.

Now you can conclude your meditation.

1. Thank God for having created you.

2. In life, make yourself available to whatever God expects of you. Look for concrete ways to offer yourself in service; this way your thoughts and ideas become reality instead of being added to a pile of unfulfilled good intentions.

3. Ask for the help of our Blessed Mother Mary—she made herself magnificently available at God's request—putting her words and thoughts into action!

Now you can conclude your meditation with the Our Father.

CHAPTER 10

Our Second Meditation— Why was I created?

You prepare for this encounter.

1. I invite you again to become aware of the Presence of God and place within His divine heart.
2. Ask the Holy Spirit and the Blessed Mother Mary to be your companions with you in prayer.

Reflect on the following points:

1. In a certain sense, God has no real need of you in order to be God. God created you freely out of love for you. God has given you many gifts:
   - Intelligence with which to think, to ponder and understand life
   - Memory, so you can recall your own life story
   - Free will, which allows you to make choices that enable you to make something beautiful of your life
   - Imagination: that power which makes you bloom with creativity
   - Sight, which opens the windows of your being, enabling you to discover this many faceted world

- A Tongue and a voice *"box"* which allow you to speak and communicate with others, and to praise God
- Potential, gifts and talents yet to be discovered on your amazing journey that can only be unveiled over time

2. If you think about all of the above gifts, you'll realize that God desires your happiness. Remember this when sadness and negative thoughts begin to overpower you. The sure knowledge of God's love and generosity will strengthen you in these moments.

3. You probably know many people who are pack rats. Their lives consist of accumulating many possessions, most of which they don't need. They attempt to impress others with all their stuff. There are others who flaunt living promiscuously as fashionable. Do you really think this makes for true and lasting happiness?

Now bring your prayer to conclusion.

1. Recall specific events, encounters, or actions of the last day or so. Did any of them seem special or different? Can you identify any particular blessing or satisfaction that came with any of them? Could this be how God lets you know that he is present to you? Looking at your life daily you will gradually become more familiar with how God is present to you always—then it will be easier for you to place your presence into God's.

2. Reconsider all those things that encumber your life: negative thoughts, useless activities, poor attitude; things that make for a constructive life.

3. Remember those times of strength that allowed you to grow and affirm yourself and to become more authentic.

Compose yourself a simple prayer...for example:

Thank you, Lord, for having given me existence and purpose. Today I want to put all that I am—my gifts and talents—my entire being at Your service. May all the hours of my life be a response of love for the magnificent gift of Your own Life, which You freely offered up for us.

CHAPTER 11

Meditation Three—
The gifts God has given you

Prepare now for your encounter.

1. I invite you to place yourself in the Presence of God.
2. Ask the Holy Spirit and the Blessed Mother Mary to accompany you in your prayer

Reflect upon the following points:

1. God has given you physical gifts. You have a totally unique body. It may be more or less agile, but it is your gift. You have the duty to take care of it in a healthy manner. You are also gifted with a family, and friends who can sustain and support you.

   Consider then all the blessings you have, especially compared with many others who suffer physically, or have disrupted family lives. Try to be grateful for what you have and pray for them. Those in different circumstances have as much value as you do. It is to your benefit to be aware always of all that you enjoy.

2. God has also given you your intellectual gifts. There are some who will never be able to read a book...or

understand an abstract concept. You are fortunate to be able develop your intelligence and put it to good use. So in a certain way you are privileged!

3. You have also had the good fortune to desire and to discover your spiritual gifts. You are a Christian and belong to a Church. You have been aided in discovering this church, perhaps in your youth or at some other time along your way. You can celebrate the sacraments. You know that your sins can be forgiven. Your God has drawn near you—or better yet, you have become aware of how near God always is to you—and this too is extremely fortunate, and a magnificent discovery for you!

You may conclude your prayer.

1. Thank God for all that you have and for this time spent with God
2. Realize that you sometimes can be self-centered and feel you are status or things—somewhat like a teenager who may at times think they only have rights and privileges, and no responsibilities.
3. Consider how you might more sincerely and deeply express gratitude for your blessings to your God.
4. Try to find a way that your gratitude might be transformed into concrete action. I invite you to make a commitment of some type that you will undertake in this spirit. (You could attend Mass, volunteer at a soup kitchen or a homeless shelter, set a regular time for personal time, scripture or spiritual reading, join a

support group for conversation about the Christian life, or maybe simplify the space in which you live). You are not limited—there is much to which you can commit. But don't be overly ambitious in the beginning or you may burn out. Set parameters to be clear about your commitment, and then be faithful to it.

5. Ask the Lord to help you to keep this resolution that you've made.

Conclude your prayer with the Our Father.

CHAPTER 12

Meditation Four— My imperfections

Prepare for your encounter.

1. I invite you to place yourself in the presence of God.
2. Ask the Holy Spirit and our Blessed Mother Mary to accompany you in your prayer.

Reflect on the following points:

1. Think about the offenses, hurts or sins—whatever you want to call them—that you may have committed. Identify faults or the negative traits that you see in yourself—your weaknesses and your frailties.
2. Consider the ingratitude you have shown to God in your self-centeredness.
3. At this point in your reflection, you may have the feeling that God only loves you for the good you do. If that's the case, you also probably think that God can hardly have any great love for a person as mediocre and filled with flaws as you sometimes feel you are. If that's your reasoning, I have to tell you that you've got it all wrong. God loves you—totally—completely —the whole pack-

age—just the way you are! Because it's not all about you, but about God who is Love itself.

4. Recall the prodigal son in the Gospel. In selfishness and self-centeredness, the son demanded his inheritance and left his father. Along the way, he wasted his inheritance, stumbled and fell until he bottomed out and was left with nothing. He finally returned home to find that the father he had disrespected and not appreciated, despite everything, <u>never</u> <u>ever</u> stopped loving him! In the same way God marvelously loves you in spite of your weaknesses. And so, like the prodigal son, are invited to leave behind all that weighs you down and run to God who <u>never</u> <u>ever</u> stops loving you!

5. Now, concretely identify and determine what you can and will do to show yourself and the Load that you are serious about changing your life.

6. Ask God, with an *Our Father*, to help you keep this resolution.

CHAPTER 13

Meditation Five—On death

You prepare for your encounter.

1. I invite you to place yourself in the Presence of God.
2. Ask the Holy Spirit and our Blessed Mother Mary to accompany you in your prayer.
3. Imagine that you are in the hospital and have been told that you are stricken with an incurable illness.

Reflect on the following points:

(This reflection on death is a bit unusual. Try to imagine that Saint Francis is talking directly to you.) *Although it is part of nature, death was very frequent in my day. It was a brutal time in history. The specter of death was always present—you saw it every day. Can you begin to imagine that you couldn't even enter a town or village without being confronted by it? It seemed as if a military force was on the move. Terrible epidemics abounded and pestilence was everywhere. There was no medicine, "magic pill" or vaccine to cure anything or add to the "quality of life." This meditation will undoubtedly be rather surprising when considered in the beginning of the twenty first century since things with regard to health care are so very different now. . That's all right.*

If this subject makes you squeamish and really uncomfortable, you may pass over this meditation and move on to the next one.

1. I invite you to consider the fact that one day your life will come to an end. Of course it is not your prerogative to know whether it will be after many years from now or in a short time. You also don't know whether it will happen by an accident or following a lingering illness. I know this idea is not very pleasing to you—but the reality is that one day your life will come to an end.

2. At that moment, it will be as if the world were coming to an end—at least for you. All the material things that you held dear will disappear forever; your car, your clothing, your house, your memberships, and all the stuff we hang on to. The old saying goes—*"you can't take it with you!"* In the end, there will remain only one thing that will last forever, and that is the <u>good</u> you have done.

3. You will undoubtedly be sad to leave this earth and your body that served you well. In a short while little memory of your time on earth will remain. When the funeral is over, there may be an engraved inscription, even a marker, but memories of you kept in minds will grow old and fade away...

4. However—something magnificent will happen when you breathe your last breath—you will breathe that last breath back to God who first breathed life into you. You will see this God—your God—face to face. God will then ask you *"What have you done with your life—your life that began with my breath!"*

5. From now on, consider how your life can be a response of love.

You may conclude your prayer with an Our Father.

CHAPTER 14

Meditation Six—
What will happen when the
savior's eyes meet your eyes?

Prepare for your encounter.

1. I invite you to place yourself in the Presence of God.
2. Ask the Holy Spirit and our Blessed Mother Mary to accompany you in your prayer.

Reflect upon the following points:

1. At the end of time, the Gospel accounts tell us that our world as we know it will disappear.
2. We become more aware that everything—every single thing that surrounds us is passing and will ultimately perish—disappear. We also know that we are called to enter into eternity—forever. We await the Resurrection of the Dead.
3. We will *"see God face to face,"* and God's great Love will glow and illuminate us from within.
4. A separation of good from bad will take place within us. The good we have done will live on.

5. We will be asked, *"How well have you loved?"* to account for our lives. Our consciences will be revealed. God will make us understand what we have done with our gift of time on earth.

6. In the Gospel, we find some truly fearsome words of condemnation. Our God respects the decision of those who have chosen to take the route of absolute evil to its logical culmination...On the other hand, for those who have attempted to take the path of good, there are some magnificent words of invitation to enter into eternal life—A life which God has prepared for us. (You can reference this in Chapter 5 of Saint Matthew's Gospel—the Beatitudes in the Sermon on the Mount.)

You may conclude your prayer.

Consider what you can do in and with the time that is given to you to concretely help make the world around you a little better. Even a small or modest attempt is a beginning.

Conclude with the *Our Father.*

CHAPTER 15

Meditation Seven—Absolute evil

You *prepare for this encounter.*

1. I invite you to place yourself in the Presence of God.
2. Ask the Holy Spirit and our Blessed Mother Mary to accompany you in your prayer.
3. Imagine a city—a city that is very dark, gritty and dirty. It is sinister and scary. It stinks—its air is polluted, a heavy reddish gray. The water in the river is yellow green and gives off a foul odor. The people living in this city shuffle with their heads cast down like prisoners. They cannot escape this foul pit of a place.

Reflect upon the following points.

1. Absolute evil exists. It is in the horror of the concentration camps of World War II—in the hatred and violence that festers in economically deprived, physically dilapidated and crowded, overpopulated sections of many cities. This is a result of selfishness and of the way humanity has trashed the liberties with which we have been gifted.

2. The loss of values, the disrespect, exploitation and denigration of others—(often those who are deemed different or the least)—the inability to accept, understand, to love, or to forgive, the escalation and glorification of violence; these equally destructive elements are even more deadly and serious than are material destruction or physical deprivation.
3. Most likely, you have had some bad experiences yourself in life—maybe from illness, failure, rejection or a host of other difficulties which life's cards may have dealt you.

You conclude your prayer.

1. Try to see whether, in your life, you might be harboring a certain attraction or fascination within that makes evil look good.
2. If you discover some shadowy areas in your life, reflect how you might best overcome them.
3. Consider what efforts you need in order to be a more effective witness to living the Beatitudes.
4. Pray for all those who are burdened by a life that seems too difficult for them to bear.

Conclude your prayer with the *Our Father.*

CHAPTER 16

Meditation Eight— Happiness

You prepare for this encounter.

1. I invite you to place yourself in the Presence of God.
2. Ask the Holy Spirit and our Blessed Mother Mary to accompany you in your prayer.

Reflect on the following points:

1. Have you ever had the experience of spending time outdoors on a beautiful summer's night? If you have, you probably allowed the awesomeness of the experience carry you off into thought—into the recesses of your mind! There are probably other wonderful memories stored away in your memories. These could be the memory of a breathtaking mountain view that causes you to stand in awe and embrace silence—just taking it in...or perhaps, there is a certain place that is very special to you.

Right now I invite you in thought, to create an interior landscape in your mind and in your heart that is made up of all that you have loved the most! Remember the happiness of just being alive that you experienced.

2. In your life's journey, you have probably met some remarkable people for whom you feel great affection and have great admiration. Think of these women and men whom you admire. You are not only attracted to what you see in their appearance but also to their interior demeanor and life that shines through—in other words—the whole package. Think of them. Think of those special moments spent with them in which you knew true and deep happiness.

3. Imagine that the Kingdom of God is a coming together of all that is beautiful, and of the complete fulfillment of being in that relationship! The limited experiences we gain in our passage through life constitute a sort of anticipation—a glimpse and foretaste so to speak—of that eternal happiness that we are promised. Now, the image that comes to my mind is that of birds winging and gliding through the air, singing for joy as they greet first sunlight. This is how I imagine limitless happiness in the full Light of God!

Now you may conclude your prayer.

The kingdom of God is not yet here, but it nevertheless has already begun. How can you begin to recognize it and seek it in a concrete way? How can you participate in the building of this kingdom? Make a practical resolution that you will be able to keep during your day to do this.

End with an *Our Father*.

CHAPTER 17

Meditation 9—
Now, which choice?

You prepare for this encounter.

1. I invite you to place yourself in the presence of God.
2. Ask the Holy Spirit and our Blessed Mother Mary to accompany you in your prayer.

Reflect on the following points:

Imagine that you are on a trip. You come to a border that represents the dividing line between absolute good and absolute evil.

1. Realize that you have limitless choices before you. God has increased your freedom to the extreme.
2. Reflect on the idea that there are eternal consequences to what you will do with your existence. Your story is already being written in that infinite dimension which God has dreamed for you.
3. God does not minimize our freedom. If there were no choice for evil in the universe, would your freedom still exist?

4. Jesus Christ sets a road with many demands before you, yet it is one that has unlimited horizons. He invites you *"come follow me."*

You can conclude your prayer.

1. I can choose to flirt with evil or I can choose to run as far from it as possible—it's a decision that has to be made.
2. I can open my heart to Christ's invitation knowing that he will carry me through difficult situations that could lead to deadly consequences.
3. I can ask if what I'm about to embark on is focused on selfishness and gratification or generosity and selflessness.
4. When I am weak, can I reach out and ask for help?

Remember the Lord, His invitation, His work and his words—*"I am with you till the end of the ages."* Look to his example and love—he will give you what you need to choose what is good— even with all its difficulties—and you will then *Live Jesus!*

End with the *Our Father.*

CHAPTER 18

Meditation Ten—
Choosing to live with your God

Prepare now for this encounter.

1. I invite you to place yourself in the Presence of God.
2. Ask the Holy Spirit and our Blessed Mother Mary to accompany you in your prayer.

Reflect on the following points:

1. Imagine that you are a journalist—a reporter covering a war-torn country. This country has been through absolute hell. Violence, unspeakable atrocities, rape and pillage; all the marks of a terrible civil war that has disfigured the landscape and desolated the social fabric. When you encounter the militia, you see in their eyes a seething hatred, the desire for vengeance and for an escalation of terror. Sporadic fighting breaks out here and there. Bodies of the dead litter the streets—men, women and little children. Off to one side, you see civilians. They lie prostrate—numb—completely crushed and demoralized by the terrifying sights and experiences they have witnessed and barely survived.

Humanity alone is responsible for what is happening. This is pure hell.

2. Now imagine that a humanitarian mission arrives. These rescuers are putting their lives at risk to save anyone and everyone they can. The personal sensitivity and generosity of these men and women is unbounded. They have left their own comfort zones, placing their talents at the service of these victims of hatred. Their actions—their example demands and brings out your most fervent esteem and admiration—they wow you.

3. You are here for the story—this one could make or break your career. Your organization wants the scoop—you want the scoop—the break—the exclusive—the most with the most danger that's going to sell the most papers and get the most hits. You can see the awards and prizes coming your way. A story about the victims invites a sensitive approach. One that chronicles the militia and their motives offers danger and excitement and an unprecedented view into this war—a career-maker. Which side do you want to be on? What choice will you make?

4. If there exists within the human psyche a mysterious desire to commit evil, if there is a strange and collective fascination to kill and destroy, there also exists an incredible power that is the complete opposite—the desire to what is constructive and life giving. This power is exampled in the *communion of saints.* Saints—ordinary people like ourselves who struggled with all aspects of being human, but didn't give up when things were

tough. The actions of all these witnesses for the good—witnesses to God—make humanity showing its best side. Do you have the courage—are you willing to enter into this circle—this dynamic?

5. Christ calls you by name, *"come follow me."* He needs you today!

You may conclude your *prayer*.

What will my decision be for today?

What will my actions be for tomorrow?

End with the *Our Father*.

CHAPTER 19

How can you change your life?

I've just presented you with a series of conversations, or meditations with your God. With these little prayer guides, I hope I have been able to help you get to know yourself and your God a little bit more. Once you have become familiar and comfortable with the dynamic of regular personal prayer, you may want to come up with some of your own.

Now, let's take the next step. I invite you to contact a priest so that you may celebrate and experience the Sacrament of Reconciliation by making an honest and open Confession. Don't be afraid of this! When someone is bitten by a poisonous snake, the person is given an antidote to save his/her life and restore health. Think of Reconciliation as being something like that. Not only can this antidote restore you, it can turn you into someone who is much more authentic, genuine, human and therefore holier than you were originally. With the mercy of God, you have confronted the poison of your sin! God is not stingy in offering mercy. God gives it to us in its totality, without reservation and without looking back. Your life and attitude will take on a whole different flavor! It's true that it takes a truck load of humility to take the first step but once you take this step, you will not regret it!

I also have to add that the action of confessing your faults, failings and sin is part of a very ancient tradition in the Church. It has lasted because it is truly liberating. If it were not—this tradition would have been discarded centuries ago.

When you meet with the priest that you've chosen to celebrate this sacrament, remember that the Lord Jesus went to the very depths of total love in order to bring us this act of pardon. He gave His Life completely until there was not more to give by embracing the Cross.

One last bit of advice: above all, do not be scrupulous by living in fear of having forgotten to mention something or not to have given all the tiny details...be humble and let honesty be your guide as you share not so much a *"list"* of sins, but more importantly the scope of the faults and sins that intimately affect, weigh down and tarnish your humanity, obstructing the direction of your life. That will be a lot!

Your spiritual guide will certainly give you some advice in response to your confession. Don't hesitate to take the time for good conversation with him. Profit from this meeting as it's a time when your Lord speaks to you personally.

At the conclusion of the Sacrament, take the time to encounter your God again in another period of personal prayer and thanksgiving. To help you get started in your prayer, I offer the following chapter.

CHAPTER 20

Prayer at the conclusion of your Reconciliation celebration

You have offered me your pardon, Lord God.

You are concerned with my welfare, even though I haven't done very much to earn it.

Here I am before you with the experience of these years that you have given me to live.

I want to be more aware of just how much you are a Faithful God.

I want to tell you, that so often, I am the one who has wandered far from Your Presence.

You loved me before I could even be aware of it.

Through my Baptism, You offered me the idea of life and happiness to which the Good News and Your Beatitudes invite me...

You have allowed me to take certain basic steps in my interior life, and I want to remember these now: my Profession of Faith, my Confirmation...

Your patience did not cast me away when I was unfaithful to what you proposed.

Yes, it's true; you are always there, with your immense love for humanity; with this gift of your own life, which says more than any words can ever express.

Here I am before you then, reconciled to you by your sacrament.

Simply, truly, I humbly ask your forgiveness.

I reaffirm my desire to follow you, despite my weaknesses.

Receive today my intention to be more faithful from this moment on.

Help me to find the desire to serve others.

Give me confidence in the resources and talents you have placed within me, so that I may accomplish it.

If it should happen that I fall once again into the sins that I am trying now to overcome, give me your hand, so that I can quickly return to the path that I set for myself. Do not allow me to fall into discouragement.

Here, Lord, are my true desires of this moment.

Be with me Lord, by your Spirit of strength and joy.

CHAPTER 21

In order to conclude this first step

I have two last points I wish to recommend to you.

The first is to pay close attention to the words of absolution, the prayer of pardon that the priest will pray at the conclusion of your confession. This prayer involves you just as much as do all the sacraments.

The second is to tell you that it might be worthwhile for you to take some time following your celebration of the sacrament to write down the commitments that you wish to make for your future as a sign of change. In this way, you can make a kind of *"personal covenant"* with your God. The advantage here is that writing it down allows you to make your thoughts concrete. This also allows you to come back to them. You can also reread them regularly as a reminder of what you have committed yourself to do. You can also reflect upon how well you are doing living your life as you review what you have written.

Without a doubt, as I've already told you, you'll find that some of the faults that you have been able to overcome will reappear at times. Don't let this discourage you. In spite of these unwished for *"wind gusts"* that sometimes come along and throw your *"sailboat"* of life off course, you can still maintain the direction you have set yourself and reach the harbor with the aid of your interior compass! But in order for you to do this, I still have some advice to give you!

CHAPTER 22

How to find those little details that can change your life

In bright daylight, it's easy to see all those little imperfections on your face: pimples, beauty marks, and blemishes...when you look into your mirror. It's somewhat similar with your spiritual life. Once you let go and allow yourself to be guided more and more by the Holy Spirit, you will eventually notice all sorts of imperfections that can be quite bothersome once you become aware of them.

Celebrating the Sacrament of Reconciliation and making an honest and open Confession are most important. If you continue to take advantage of this sacrament, it will help you reinforce your desire to identify and avoid the most outstanding faults that occur in your life.

If your life were to exhibit a fundamental pattern of lying and cheating, a serious problem would exist. You would have to take this to heart and deal with it so you could live a healthier lifestyle. You would have to start over—begin again—and that will be work.

On the other hand, if you occasionally say some things that are not exactly true, either because you are joking with your friends, you think exaggeration is humorous, or simply to please someone, you'll agree that that is not very serious. However, if these are *"little"* lies, have become habitual, or to be very direct with you, if your habit of not being precise and attentive in your words leads to some problems...it's better to correct the situation quickly.

Occasionally, on a beautiful summer's day, you have certainly must have had the opportunity to eat outdoors. You probably have experienced some flies landing in your glass or pop can and drowning themselves. Unpleasant as this thought is, you may even have swallowed one of them when taking a sip of your drink. In reality, that's not very serious and the consequences are minimal. However if that fly were to be a wasp, swallowing it would be dangerous and could have serious, even deadly consequences.

A little fly is not too appetizing or appealing. In reality the little insect will hardly cause any damage to you or your drink. You can fish it out and throw it away easily enough. And should you find several of them in your beverage you'll probably lose all desire to drink it.

In the same way, these little faults end up causing some upset in our lives.

Sometimes it happens that spiders come along and spin their webs in messy beehives. It's not really dangerous for the bees that are strong enough to get themselves out from these sticky webs when they become trapped. But it does disrupt them from living an orderly life in the beehive. It's the same thing with all those annoying habits we have. They end up preventing or disrupting us from orienting ourselves in the direction of serving God and others. However getting rid of those habits is not beyond our capacity or capability.

A *"white lie"*, a *"dirty look"*, a *"slight"* exaggeration, or misuse of our time; these things are not all that serious as long as we act like our bees do and make sure to chase the spiders with their stick webs away. If we let these little faults have their way with us, like the spider's web, the risk of becoming trapped becomes very real.

Let me say once again that it is not a case of depriving yourself of all sorts of things that seem very appealing to you. Rather it is because you have become aware of the Love God has for you. It's because you want to respond ever more generously to this love in your life.

CHAPTER 23

Be careful of the choices you make

Sports, free time, evenings with friends, meals out at a restaurant, stylish clothing, movies, late nights dancing or hanging out in a bar; none of this harmful in and of itself. These things can be good or bad depending on how you approach them. Allowing yourself to become so obsessed with them to the point of living only for them is to live a life without any real depth. You exist only on the surface of yourself—in a very superficial way. I repeat; spending a night in a dance hall, working out, taking care of your *"image,"* are all things that are perfectly compatible with the life of a young Christian, but to let them become the be all and end all of your existence—taking way too much pleasure in them can quickly become dangerous. What's bad is not in doing these things, but actually liking and doing them to excess—turning them into little *"gods."*

It's unfortunate if these are the only types of activities you cultivate in your life. You deserve better. To fill your life completely with a *"hip"* culture—a popular *"in the moment"* culture—a culture or pursuit that offers little genuine productivity is shallow and shortsighted. It allows you to be used and exploited by others for their gain. In short, it shorts you by not letting you make the best use of your potential.

It's been said that in the early tradition of the people of Israel they chose to abstain not only from alcohol, but they also gave up eating grapes. There was hardly any chance for them to become drunk on grapes, but it seems that they feared becoming too fond of them and developing a desire to drink wine...I don't think you have to go quite that far...but it is important to become quite conscious and understand that there are consequences to the choices that you make.

Deer that have overeaten are forced to go and hide themselves in the deepest thickets because they know that in the open field, if they were hunted, they would not be able to flee to safety. If your heart is loaded down with an overabundance of activities, you will have trouble catching up with God—even if you try to sprint.

I bet you've noticed that little children love to chase butterflies...they find this thrilling. No one would want to prevent them from playing this little game. On the contrary, adults find it cute. However if an adult were to act in the same way, people would take notice. They would wonder about his maturity and feel sorry for him. If it happens often enough some may even have doubts about his mental stability. You don't need me to spell this out for you; you can judge for yourself what you should do. I invite you to look closely at how you use your time and energy, and to decide what is most important—what really matters in your life.

CHAPTER 24

And those annoying little habits

It's not so much our faults, but those annoying little habits that we have can make it painful for others to deal with us. Some of us are inclined to be a bit depressed. Sometimes we can appear to be quite negative. There are others who can have an exasperating exuberance. And still others are closed up and are not very communicative. You'll also notice that some people are naturally inclined be more explosive in their temperament while others are inclined to be overly enthusiastic. No one—I repeat—NO ONE IS PERFECT! However there is nothing wrong with trying to temper our nature a bit. As a result of working on ourselves, we can end up really changing ourselves. The key here is to be compassionate toward ourselves as well as with others! This is good self-care.

Over the years fruit farmers have been able to figure out how to graft trees. Doing this allows the improved trees to produce much better fruit than would be possible without human intervention. Why don't we do the same thing with ourselves? I have a personal tidbit to share with you! In my youth I had a real inclination to anger and I struggled with it. Because of my struggle, I also recognized that the idea of working on myself is quite possible. In fact, this is one of the key subject areas that I'm going to address in the following chapters!

PART TWO

*Elevating your heart and
soul to God*

CHAPTER 1

It's important to make time in your life for personal prayer

It's my hope that by now you've developed a little taste for personal prayer. Now that you've tried it, I'd like to offer you some practical advice about the subject. I want you to consider what I say with complete freedom of your spirit. With a little practice, I'm sure you are able easily to identify what suits you personally, and you will ultimately become you own best advisor on the subject.

When you sit outside in the sun for a while, and if you're careful, you begin to notice that your skin starts to tan. It turns a nice bronze color. Well, by exposing yourself to your God in times of personal prayer, you will likewise be transformed. This will be a completely invisible and interior transformation. These encounters with God will be like the heat of sunlight that warms and illumines your soul, or like a river that will irrigate and nourish your interior thirst. Your inner life will be fortified.

Yes, I heartily advise you to take time regularly for a *"heart to heart"* with God in the deepest recesses of your being. You see, it's by being in God's presence regularly that you allow God to sculpt and fashion you into something more wonderful. Christ Jesus said that He is the Light for a reason. Let yourself be enlightened by Him!

You know, a little child, after babbling and stuttering and making all sorts of sounds eventually begins to speak. Over time it ends up learning the language of its parents quite naturally by imitating their accents and intonations. By giving time to the Lord in very simple and intimate conversation, over time, you too will end up speaking God's language interiorly.

I'd also like to emphasize this point: personal prayer is a door. Don't hesitate to open it often. The Lord became one like us to share our humanity and our journey. He is near to you at all times. In turn, try to find a way to be near to him yourself.

This moment of encounter with your God will depend on how available you make yourself. Some people like the mornings; others, the evenings. Just make sure that the time you set aside for God is long enough.

Some people prefer to pray at home and others in a park. Some people prefer their personal prayer time in a church. It's a place where there may not be any interruptions. However, today, many churches are closed except for daily and Sunday mass or some other special occasions such as weddings and funerals. So it may be hard to find one that is available. If there is one that stays open for a few hours each day it's worth the try. In light of this situation, you may have to find a practical place or space near you that is quiet and has an atmosphere of calm that would be conducive to your prayer experience. We are lucky that our ability to connect with God is not limited by time or space. We can pray anywhere at any time! Nevertheless, the point I'm trying to make is to urge you to find someplace that is quiet and without distraction.

Always begin your personal time by becoming aware of the Presence of God within you. Ask God to help you enter into prayer. To help you to do this, you can begin with some prayers that are very familiar: for example, the prayer Jesus gave us, the *Our Father*. Many like to say a *Hail Mary* or pray the Rosary as a way to prepare for deeper prayer. It's simple and yet beautiful. The repetition of this prayer creates a relaxing inner landscape that will be helpful in getting you ready for your encounter. Still other people like to read a passage from the Bible, a favorite book, a psalm, or perhaps even a poem. And still others may look at an icon, photograph or picture of some inspirational art, listen to music or a song, or even view a short video clip. Saying prayers, reading a passage, looking at a picture or video and listening to music are not the end, but rather a means to a much deeper interior encounter to which you are being invited.

If you forget your prayer time or have to put it off because of obligation you have, or something comes up on a particular day, try to do it later on hat same day—even if only for a little while. Just avoid an overly long period of reflection that could become a distraction to your good intentions. The important thing is to *"Just do it!"*

CHAPTER 2

A little technique to help you to begin your personal prayer encounter with your God

If you start to read many books about personal prayer, they often make it out to seem easy—almost effortless! The author will say, as I have—*"Put yourself in the Presence of God."*

Do you find this easy? I sure don't—I'm in the same boat as you are. From my personal experience I'd like to offer four ideas to help you. I've found that they have helped me a lot.

Here's the first one. Try to become aware that your God is Present <u>everywhere</u>. Birds although not conscious of it, are enveloped by air wherever they fly. In the same way, even though we are not conscious of it, the Presence of God totally envelops our lives. This is the unseen reality and you know this—at least theoretically. By becoming aware of God's presence, we become more in tune with our surroundings and ourselves.

A blind person attending a formal dinner with his congressman could forget quite easily where he is because he can't see his environment or those surrounding him. He could end up forgetting his manners and eat sloppily. But if you, or someone who can see attends the same dinner, you'd try to remember your manners, and you would certainly take your cue by observing those dining with you.

You know, we're often like our blind person. We forget the Presence of God because we can't see God. My point is that it's helpful to be sensitive to <u>all</u> that surrounds us and adjust our awareness to this reality.

Pray and get to know the following passage from Psalm 138:

Lord, You have searched me, and You know me.

You know when I sit and when I stand.

If I climb to the highest heavens, You are there.

Where can I hide from Your Spirit?

From Your Presence, where can I flee?

If I fly with the wings of the dawn and land beyond the sea,

Even there Your Hand will guide me.

Your right Hand holds me fast.

Even darkness is not dark for You.

Probe me, Lord, and know my heart; try me, know my concerns.

See if my way is crooked, then lead me in the ancient pathways.

My second idea invites you to be aware that God is not only everywhere, but that God is most particularly

within you. Scripture proclaims this and tells you where—
"*In your heart*"—"*In your mind.*" Ask yourself these questions.
What makes up your personality? Why do you smile the
way you do? Why do you like to dress the way you do, like
the music you do, or like the sports you play? Why do you
think your particular thoughts and how do you fuse them
together so quickly to create an idea? Why do you carry
yourself, speak, or react the way you do? All of these questions probe at aspects of your totality—physical,
mental, personality and character traits. Together these
questions force you to look inside at the big picture and see
glimpses of yourself. You become more aware of who you
are and what you are all about. Well now, if you take little
glimpses into your environment, you just may begin to see
God's presence in those surroundings. If God is present in
them, then God is just as present in all the little aspects and
preferences that make you the person you are.

The third idea will remind you that your God looks
on you in a most special way when you are in prayer. The
person who is praying—trying to speak and to listen to
God becomes better, and the relationship (much like our
human relationships) blooms to become deeper, more life
giving and fulfilling within God's intimate gaze.

There is a wonderful love story in the Bible called
The Song of Songs. The young girl in the story becomes
aware of the gaze of her beloved who contemplates the totality of her beauty through the window. The love she has
for her beloved grows much deeper and becomes more
beautiful. God contemplates you in this same way—the

relationship will grow deeper and your prayer will make you more beautiful.

In the fourth idea, I want you to use your imagination. Imagine that Jesus is seated right next to you as a true and faithful friend. If you are praying in a church, His presence is not just in your imagination. Your faith will tell you that he is really there, particularly in the Holy Eucharist, which is reserved in the tabernacle of the church.

If you are not praying in a church, rest assured. He is present in your heart as well.

Like I said at the beginning, these four ideas come from my own experience. They work different ways at different times. Try one as a way of *"putting yourself in the Presence of God."* Don't spend all your time in this first phase of prayer. Just be aware of the attitude with which you approach and begin your encounter with your God.

CHAPTER 3

The first words are the hardest

Once you've become aware of the Presence of your God, I advise you to make a leap of faith and speak directly to your God, much in the same way you would speak to me. I bet you've had an experience like this: when we have to speak before an important group of people, the first words are always the hardest to say. We are reluctant, we feel intimidated, ill at ease, a little shy. We may even ask ourselves—What if I make a mistake? Once we start speaking, we seem to calm down a bit and our words begin to flow. The important thing is to start speaking!

Try it! Make the leap of faith.

Talk to your God.

"My eyes are fixed on you, Lord, like the eyes of a servant on the hands of his master." This is a great line from one of the Psalms. It can serve as a jumping off point to begin your conversation!

CHAPTER 4

Use the Bible—Give a Biblical image to your prayer

After having become aware of the presence of your God and beginning your conversation, I suggest that you next choose a passage from the Gospel. Once you've chosen a passage, use your imagination to build the scene. Insert yourself into the scene. Let it become real for you. Let this be a way Jesus can become closer to you.

As an example, you can recreate the image of the desert in which Jesus spent forty days in prayer. You can imagine yourself walking with him and taking in the sunrise, the changing play of light on the hillsides and the quiet and cool of the night. You can also create a scene like a movie director or videographer. A crowd comes to hear Jesus on a hillside. Place yourself in the middle of that crowd—you experience an astonishing miracle. Loaves and fishes are multiplied—everyone is fed and satisfied. You've been fed too! When he is finished, you watch him get into a boat and disappear into the fog on the Sea of Galilee.

Choosing a Gospel passage is an idea that may interest you if you enjoy a story and like to visualize things.

However if this proves difficult for you and seems a bit contrived or empty, don't go any further with it. It's an aid to help you reach your goal of conversation with your God. There are other methods that you may prefer and that may help.

CHAPTER 5

Take the time to savor the Biblical text you choose

Whether you use your imagination or not, in any case, take the time to really reflect upon and digest the passage you've chosen for the day from the Bible.

This is important—read your passage slowly.

When an idea, an impression, or an intuition crosses your mind, stop for a moment. Explore that thought. Be like a miner who has just discovered a vein of gold. The miner takes time to look at it and figure out the best approach to extracting the most gold from the vein. You can also do what bees do. They don't leave a flower until they've extracted every drop of nectar. When it seems that you've spent enough time on one idea or impression, move on to something else. Quietly continue reading your passage until you come to its conclusion. Above all, really take your time while doing this.

CHAPTER 6

Your prayer should have its effect

You've spent time with your Gospel passage. You've reflected on various ideas and intuitions you've had. Often our initial impressions or inspirations become more profound when we take time to be with them. However the good we have just experienced can be lost if we just let it sit there. I invite you to transform your experience into actions.

Here's an example. Look at the passage you've just prayed. Did you see Jesus impassioned by his encounter with all those people who crossed his path? Was he energized? Did His actions bring about more good?

Ask yourself the following questions—answer them in your heart. Is it enough to applaud and thank God for being God? Is there something more? What about me? What about my own life? Am I attentive and impassioned by my own encounter with others? How can I live and feel the passion Jesus lived and felt? What action can I take to give more character to my Christian call?

CHAPTER 7

We need to know when to stop praying

All good things come to an end, and this includes our prayer. I'm going to suggest three points you can practice when the time you've set aside for your personal prayer is finished.

- First, remember to thank your God for any inspiration you have received.
- Then thank God for giving you the many blessings, big and little, with which you are surrounded.
- Lastly, ask God's help to keep any resolutions you have made.

When we leave a gorgeous garden, we often feel it would be great if we could continue the experience and bring a few of the beautiful flowers home with us. By doing this, we can savor the rich perfume of the garden for a longer time. Act in the same way regarding your prayer— carry a few of your prayer thoughts with you throughout your day. Like the scent of those flowers, your prayer thoughts will perfume your day gently reminding you of your experience.

Here's another example. When someone goes on a trip, they often pick up a little memento to remind them of their experience. Think of your prayer thought as such a souvenir.

I've also noticed that there's something amusing regarding this subject. Many times out of habit we associate our thoughts and ideas with the place where we had them. So during the day, if you are near the place where you spent your prayer time you'll see that your thoughts born in that place will pleasantly come back to you!

CHAPTER 8

And after prayer?

Now, try not to quickly forget those resolutions you've made. They are good and beautiful. If you've decided to be more patient with certain people, then don't avoid them if you should run into them and above all pray for them.

During your day, for as long as possible, try to keep the attitude or demeanor that came from your encounter with God, but make an effort as well to move quickly from prayer to those actions that demand your attention. If you work in business, don't remain half in prayer while in a meeting, tracking the ups and downs of the stock exchange, interviewing new personnel, or planning a major sales pitch. If you are doing something less intense, vacuuming the floor, washing dishes, folding laundry, and you find yourself drifting off in a blur of thought, don't confuse this daydream with what's called contemplation. (Contemplation is a very deep form of prayer that usually develops or comes to us after a period of time—often after long living a life anchored in prayer.) Pay attention to what you are doing no matter how simple or mundane, otherwise you may have to redo everything. However, if the feeling of the

Presence of God returns to you during the course of the day, greet your God gladly in that moment—but quietly, and without show!

It hardly takes any time, in fact, in only a split second you can once again become aware that you are beneath the gaze of your God—whom you just encountered personally during your formal prayer time.

CHAPTER 9

What if you don't feel capable of praying?

If you don't feel capable of praying—realize that you are not alone. Be patient with yourself and pray anyway! It's not always going to be easy. We often look for the big or easy experience. When we don't have that, we don't think we are capable of anything else. We sometimes see ourselves as diminished—*"bit part"* actors not amounting to much in our encounter with God. But that's not true. Look at it this way. Some of the greatest movies ever made had need of many *"extras"* in very small parts. Their presence helped make the film great. The movie couldn't be made without them. So even if you feel incapable, that your part is small, or you don't sense closeness to your God, make the effort anyway, and you will be surprised. God will know what to do and will draw near to you. Your effort is important. Remember that running away from what you feel or giving up is never the way to resolve difficulties.

CHAPTER 10

The morning

Morning is often a special time of the day. It can be quiet and uncluttered. Your prayer early in the day is a privileged time for your personal encounter with your God.

- It's the time of a fresh start. All is new again. It's a blank page in your life on which to write. Thank God for your new day!

- Take a couple of minutes and place before God what you plan to do with this new day.

- Prepare yourself interiorly in mind and heart for what you are going to experience. You may quickly think of negative things that are going to happen; of painful encounters that you may expect. Think of how you can live out these moments as positively as possible. Think of how you could witness your Christian commitment as an example for others.

- Ask your God to be with you in all those moments to come. Tell God of your trust.

These little ideas won't take you too long, and this spiritual *"conditioning"* or *"training"* can give you the energy you need for your day that's ready to unfold!

CHAPTER 11

The evening

Before or after dinner, take a few minutes for a short spiritual review. It's a *"checking in"* with your God!

- Thank God for this day.

- Go back to the beginning of the day, and do a *"fast forward"* of each hour since morning.

- Thank your God for anything positive that you were able to accomplish. Also, examine the less positive aspects of your day for any wrong you may have done. This gives you the awareness to correct your faults.

- Open your prayer to any other important situations or events that you have become aware of during your day. You may have received a call or a text message from a friend. There also may be world events, town happenings, stories you've seen on television or read about in the paper or on-line that caught your attention.

- Think of your spiritual review this way. God's Presence is always surrounding you. In the morning, you opened the window of your interior life to God's presence. In the evening you close it again. After reviewing your day and being mindful of the joys, sorrows, and worries of the world, it is time to slow down and rest.

CHAPTER 12

Little encounters with your God

When a young man falls in love with a girl, he thinks of her regularly during the day. Sometimes he becomes distracted with these thoughts.

My hope is that the thought of God will not prove too much of a distraction for you. But I'd be quite happy if it comes back to you for a few minutes several times during your day.

Most birds make nests for themselves in sheltered or cozy places. This allows them rest and to hatch their eggs in peace. Deer take refuge in thick bushes where they can feel safe. Inhospitable, unwelcoming mountains are filled with little hidden places in which to take refuge. In the same manner as these examples, you too can take a few moments of *"interior silence"* or *"refuge"* wherever you are— subway, grocery store, waiting room, classroom, lab, and sports stadium, or on a run—there are no limits!

CHAPTER 13

A passing thought

When you are busy and seem involved in of all sorts of activity, it's possible to take a quick break and reach out to your God. This interior action can give you a moment of rest and some renewed energy as you continue on with your day. When you go for a bike ride, take a hike, or work out, you often don't want to stop for anything. But it's good to take that moment's rest and a sip from your water bottle. You also may have noticed that when a little child is frightened, that child will often reach out a hand to his or her parent for reassurance. In a large crowd, this small gesture will go unnoticed. It's the same when you take that moment for your God—it goes unnoticed but can offer you that pause for refreshment you may need in the midst of your activities.

Don't try to make up all sorts of wordy prayers that you will have to force yourself to recite. Be creative—relax—and let your heart speak. In doing so, the spontaneity will prove to be a deep inexhaustible well. You may even remember some words from a favorite song or a poem that will pop into your head and inspire you. The important thing is that you take advantage of that moment.

Young lovers never stop calling one another on the phone, or sending text messages to each other. They may even do something more old fashioned—and carve their names or initials with a heart and arrow into the bark of a tree for others to see! Try to do the same with your God whose loving presence you've discovered. Reach out with little messages at different times during your day—and let your loving relationship with God be seen by others through the way you carve out your life!

I once heard a beautiful story about a fellow named Gregory. While walking along a beach one day, Gregory, who had lots of reasons to be depressed, noticed the little shells that were being pushed ashore by the waves. They would be tossed and spat out of the water in all directions resting for a moment at the water's edge, only to be engulfed again by the wavy turmoil. They appeared and disappeared in endless succession—always being battered by their surroundings. A little farther down the beach, there were big rocks and they weren't budged. These presented Gregory with an image of solidity and stability. From his experience, Gregory made the following prayer.

"Save me, my God, for the waters have penetrated deep within me; the storm has submerged me."

Gregory's observation enabled him to reach out to his God in that moment and ask for the help he needed in his life. For us as well, every little observation can become a simple living prayer.

The Church celebrates this Gregory as Saint Gregory Nazianzen.

CHAPTER 14

Appreciating the Holy Eucharist

Just as the sun rises giving Earth light, warmth, and energy, so too, the Mass is the sun of prayer. The prayer of Mass transforms us more than any other—our God becomes one within us—to enlighten us, warm us, and energize us with His love. There is nothing greater than this! I don't know if we always appreciate that. Do you know that in many countries in our world, it is extremely difficult to attend or participate in this great sacrament? There are all sorts of reasons for this—culture, politics, and sometimes a great distance. We're lucky! For us, there are many opportunities available to celebrate and live this magnificent sacrament. Let's take advantage of this wonderful gift as often as we can.

It is probably counterproductive to approach Mass with a *"what-will-I-get-out-of-it"* approach, which is so tempting. Instead, try to bring a posture of worship, being in the divine presence together with others. Offer your whole self to the Father in union with Jesus. Let yourself be transformed by the Holy Spirit and the Body and Blood of Christ, pouring out your heart, and letting God embrace and love you. Ironically, you are liable to reap far greater benefits if you go there to DO something rather than to expect to be passively gifted. I think you will find that you more and more will be becoming what you eat—that is, the Body of Christ.

CHAPTER 15

Other powerful moments

Finally, if you're attentive, you'll see that the opportunities to pray with others are much more numerous than you would ever think. It is a great blessing to be able to share and express your faith by sharing your prayer with them.

Different places, locations and even styles of prayer offer a multitude of possibility for you to pray and to connect with others. Again, take advantage of these opportunities as they can be helpful—if not you can move on to something else. The importance of praying with others helps us remember that an isolated Christian is often a Christian in danger.

CHAPTER 16

Other heavenly helpers

Mary, the Blessed Mother of Jesus, can help you in your prayer. Jesus gave her to us to be our mother as well. She is always available to us and gently invites us to open our hearts to God with confidence and in simplicity.

Many times in the Bible we find that the will of God is announced to men and women through the presence or voices of angels. These messengers are sent by God to guide and protect us. Pierre Favre, a Savoyard like me (that is, from Savoy), was one of the first members of the Jesuits. Pierre was strong, a man of the mountains, and was in no way silly or naïve. He loved to pray to the angels. This custom of his became his legacy and has been maintained for many years in France. Place yourself in the care of the angels just like Pierre and so many people in the scripture, and they will watch over your every step.

We have a special relationship with our patron saints whose names we bear. They watch over us and also help us in our prayer. We may feel there are other saints who are good examples and whom we admire because some aspect of their lives touch or intersect with ours. Forming a friendship that crosses time and eternity with these special people can inspire us and enrich our encounters with God.

CHAPTER 17

You are invited to be attentive

Lastly, there are many instances or circumstances that I can foresee when it will be necessary for you to be most attentive to your surroundings. Be aware what is happening and what you experience. I would ask you to be very focused when you have the opportunity to read, or hear a passage from the Bible. Summon all your energy, for these passages are not any ordinary words—this is the Word your God is speaking to you in that moment. Listen carefully and try not to let what you hear become quickly lost in the middle of all your daily activities and distractions.

Also, I'd like to remind you of the types of people who are invited to participate often in the Holy Eucharist:

- Those who are already perfectly <u>strong</u>, because they have reached this mark and it would be wrong to deprive themselves of the Eucharist, which can only make them better and stronger.

- Those who are <u>weak</u> and far from being strong, because it is the Eucharist, the Bread of Life that will nourish and strengthen them making them better people. The sick need a doctor more than those who are already strong and healthy. The busier you are, and the more things you have to do, the more important Mass will be in providing the *"vitamins"* you need to maintain your spiritual health.

Many years ago, it was believed that the little white rabbits living in our mountains became white because they ate the snow. This we know isn't true...but the image is much too beautiful for me to resist using. As a result of carving out and making a place within you for your God—welcoming and receiving your God in the Eucharist—you will be profoundly changed. You will be totally transformed, starting with your interior and you will begin to glow on your exterior as well.

PART THREE

Going Further…

Part three will be dedicated primarily to questions which have often been posed in my classes…Each chapter is more or less independent of the others, although certain themes may occasionally reoccur spontaneously as our conversation unfolds. I'd like to advise you to regard these passages as a friendly exchange and not as a scholarly work. If a subject doesn't particularly interest you, go on to the next one like bees do when it comes to flowers…Each chapter will be introduced by a question somewhat like those young people might ask when they are ready to learn.

CHAPTER 1

What kinds of choices should we make?

As we begin this first chapter in a new section, I'd like to cite my bees again as an example...I know this won't be surprising to you, will it? Have you ever had the opportunity to witness a swarm of bees on the move? If so, you know that the queen never leaves the hive alone. Her entire court of workers always surrounds her. Well, I think of love and generosity as being somewhat like the queen bee...when love and generosity flood the heart they are surrounded by a whole court of other virtues, which they immediately put to work.

In a sense we can compare it to a program conducted for soldiers by their commanding officers. They are repeatedly and quickly trained to react immediately to any situation at hand. However, the work of acquiring and developing virtue is not done quickly in one fell swoop, or on a hard and fast schedule, but in God's good time. The Bible describes it this way in a beautiful psalm. *"The just man is like a tree planted by the running waters, who bears fruit in due season."* When generosity and love irrigate the interior life, the fruit is produced when the time is right. The *"just"* person described repeatedly in the Bible is one who takes a <u>risk</u>—for example, saving the life of someone who is endangered by war, and who by doing so, saves the whole of humanity. The Just person not only speaks out against injustice, but also seeks to alleviate it in all its various forms—sometimes with their very life. But I must stress this point—it can't happen overnight but only at an opportune time.

Do you feel inspired to dance by different types of contemporary music that you like? Whether it be country, classic rock, rap, or reggae, and whether you like it soft or loud, I'm sure you would realize that it would be inappropriate for you to play that kind of music in a home where a family is in mourning. Think about it!

I use this as an example to help explain a fault I sometimes see in some people. Their practice of virtue becomes somewhat wearing and grating. They want to practice it constantly wherever they are. If they think a Christian should be happy, they are trying to be bubbly and forcing themselves into a rather heavy and somewhat silly state of euphoria. If on the other hand, they may be doing some sort of penance or serious self-denial, they put on long faces that make everyone uncomfortable and want to flee their company. In addition, when they allow themselves to preach to others, believing that they alone are the bearers of truth, they become real walking disasters and sow seeds of disillusion.

I say no to the above. You see, Charity must take precedence—a place of prime importance—in human relationships. We must be happy with those who are happy and know how to mourn with those who mourn according to the advice of Saint Paul in his Letter to the Romans (12:15). *"Rejoice with those who rejoice, and weep with those who weep. Have the same regard for one another; do not be haughty, but associate with the lowly; do not be wise in your own estimation."*

There are some virtues that are universally appreciated. You probably know that the Bible offers us a list of them. Among these, fortitude (the strength and courage modeled by the martyrs) is not one that you will need to practice every day. But kindness, honesty, and simplicity can give a gospel flavor and orientation to your life. Certainly, there are other more spectacular virtues, but let's begin with these simple ones. Here is another example. Sugar is complex and tastier than salt to your tongue, but simple salt is more commonly used when we are at table. So the idea here is for you to make a little collection for yourself of those simple qualities or virtues that will always be appreciated.

I think it is all right to search for the virtues that you wish to develop—this is entirely up to you. To be more specific, I'd like you to take into consideration the situation in which you find yourself now, rather than what you would prefer. Some contemplative religious (monks and nuns who may live in a monastery) feel an extraordinary call to silence. They find God in living their lives as hermits. That call would be out of place for a doctor or a human resources director. Each person's work and place, then, requires him or her to develop certain particular virtues...These will not be the same for a person in politics and a bishop, or for a military officer and the mother of a family or a baseball player and a nurse. All however, are called to appropriate and develop gospel virtues and put them into practice.

Having said that, it's better to develop true inner virtues than to be concerned with outward appearances. I'm thinking of a comet that recently passed through our sky. It seemed to fill a huge area of the heavens. However, it quickly disappeared, and what remained were the little stars...that comet seemed so big because it was close to us. But it didn't last—the stars so small, but they endured. Some virtues are like comets. We may have a sudden great concern for the homeless at the beginning of winter and this is good. However, it doesn't always last long, and usually disappears or fades away by spring. Being continually and readily available to a friend who has a tendency toward depression is something different—you tend to stick with it because of the bonded relationship. Giving up sweets, soda, television, or another favorite pastime during Lent is a good idea, but treating someone kindly who gets on your nerves all year long is much better. Continuously watching that you do not put down someone who can't do something as well as you can—not judging or mocking someone when you are tempted to by what you consider their stupidity—that's something that's a lot more enduring and character building.

It's not always the most visible action that is the best one. Little efforts repeated many times often have the same kind of power as the waves of an ocean or great lake that ultimately wear away towering cliffs along the shore. So my advice is this: choose some starting points to work on that stand out for you in your home and work environments. Don't choose too many. This is what the great witnesses to God through the years have done. They worked to develop one particular virtue, one strong point that made them exemplary. For Mother Teresa of Calcutta, it was compassion; for St. Theresa of Lisieux, it was to burn with love in her extraordinary fidelity to prayer. The Church celebrates saints who were kings, and others who were "tramps." St. Francis of Assisi loved Lady Poverty to the point that he stripped himself of all his clothing one night. St Dominic, on the other hand was an intellectual...In short, some of these witnesses developed virtues of attending to the poorest of the poor, others gave their all to intellectual research, and others were builders or lawgivers. They are all ordinary people whose practice of virtue made them extraordinary.

I once saw an extremely beautiful piece of fabric...it was woven with a great variety of threads with a seemingly wide pallet of color in a multitude of shades. Each color was in wonderful harmony with the other and I could hardly take my eyes off of it. I found this experience fascinating. This is how I see the Church. No one can develop all of the virtues. One thread cannot contain all the many nuances of all the colors available. But the weaving of many complimentary threads produces something—a tapestry—that is really magnificent.

Can you handle one last point on this subject? Once you identify your primary fault, the one that always seems to drag you down, try if possible to develop the corresponding or opposing virtue.

I've already told you that it serves no purposed to become discouraged, nervous, or distressed over your fault...it's much better to take some pleasure in gradually developing the opposite virtue. In time, doing this will give you the light of insight into your fault letting you view it as you might view a coin when you turn it from heads to tails.

I've already told you about my own personal issue with my tendency toward anger. The meekness I'm striving for doesn't have anything to do with being soft...neither does it mean going around whimpering, or with my head stuck in the clouds. The Gospel tells us that the meek are those who know how to be present to those who are suffering, and we can't do that unless we are aware or our own tendencies and weaknesses. The meek don't force themselves or their opinions on others. They respect other's opinions as well as their own. They remain faithful to themselves and to God, and do not let their violent or destructive instincts bring them down.

In my hometown, there are many wild boars. They can be heard at night sharpening their tusks; they rub them against their other teeth and all at once, everything becomes sharp—the teeth as well as the tusks. Something similar happens to our virtues. In developing the one that you think is most necessary, you'll find that the others will become more focused and refined.

In the Bible, we have the story of Job, a man who received an avalanche of every type of evil imaginable as a result of being the object of a bet between God and the devil. This was originally intended to develop his patience. His entire attitude became exemplary in every way as he endured these experiences. God himself in this story admired Job's virtues of discernment and trust. Mother Teresa of Calcutta devoted her life to caring for the elderly, dying, and poorest of the poor—in short—many who are rejected by society. In doing so she developed deep compassion and its related virtues modeling the reality of sainthood.

CHAPTER 2

Making choices (continued)

St. Augustine, who was a convert to Catholicism after having gone through many life experiences that he found troubling, and which he would later regret, points out that those who throw themselves into the spiritual life with great determination have often committed certain youthful indiscretions or transgressions. Their new behavior shows a very positive disposition, but the attitude that they sometimes adopt can be excessive. I am referring basically to what we call *"scruples:"* in other words, they are suffering from such great concern about their behavior—past and especially the present—that every action plunges them into an abyss of agony. The fear of doing the wrong thing and *"displeasing God"* becomes exaggerated to the point where it is unhealthy. This way of thinking can become a veritable form of slavery.

The example of St. Bernard on this subject is very interesting. In the beginning, this young nobleman was quite a fiery youth, but extremely disciplined. His gifts of leadership called him when he was young to the post of abbot in a new monastery. He was terribly demanding of his brother monks, who were young like himself. He explained to them that they had to renounce all worldly goods—completely! When he heard their confessions, he completely demoralized them by his harsh observations and the severity of his advice. You can imagine the effect this had. It was pretty disastrous. Unwittingly, St. Bernard ultimately discouraged these young men completely as they strove to live their religious ideals.

However, as you can see, although St. Bernard's strictness sprang from an admirable ideal of Christian perfection—it was just carried out way too far. Medieval tradition tells us that God Himself appeared to this young, overly strict priest abbot in order to set him straight. Suddenly, St. Bernard changed completely; He apologized to his companions, and the quality of his relationship to them and his leadership became so agreeable that his influence became extraordinary.

We can also look at the example of St. Pauline. This young woman was extremely demanding of herself. Her penance and self-depravation became so extreme that she went into an alarming state of physical decline. Her bishop had to take her to task because of this, while at the same time he observed that in others, her faults would have to be considered virtues! Let's take a positive outlook regarding those who are trying to do their best, even if they are not right on target yet...and as for ourselves, lets try to avoid excess.

If you often get a chance to read different types of religious literature, you'll find the sharing of some very powerful spiritual experiences that certain people have, even today. You'll see that they discuss some quite unusual phenomena, such as apparitions, the stigmata, visions and ecstasies...in my opinion; these are not what we should be seeking. It seems that God produces exceptional signs such as these in certain people, which are a kind of anticipation of future perfection. These special gifts are not virtues, but rather an exceptional gift or present given to a person by God. We can regard them as little samples of the future *"transfiguration"* or transformation to which everyone is called. That being said, I repeat again, don't seek such experiences. They are not at all necessary for living your life as a young Christian. You can love your God without having the intensity of those spiritual experiences. In any case, it's not something that can be brought about by your own desire or by any particular series of events.

So my best advice to you is that you just be yourself, and that you pay attention to the gifts you have that are at your disposal: patience, availability, purity of intention, compassion, simplicity, attempting to correct your faults, and seeking a regular time for encountering your God in your daily life. Let's freely leave extraordinary mystical phenomena to those who are true mystics. In this way, we will be the *"worker bees"* of the spiritual life, reminding ourselves that not everyone can be the personal confidant of the boss! For all of the rest of us, we can clearly see in the Gospels that the Master does not reward us according to the importance of the role we play or the job we have, but by considering the love we have and the intention with which it is lived out.

There's an amusing passage in the Bible where Saul, the first king of Israel is seen searching for his father's donkeys, which have escaped their pens. This work certainly couldn't be considered prestigious in any way. However, it was when looking for those donkeys that he crossed the path of the prophet Samuel who had been expressly charged by God to recruit the future king. So it was while engaging in the noble work of searching for donkeys, that Saul became king of his nation! So then let's learn here and try not to be pretentious. Those who would like to pass themselves off for angels are often not even simple honest folk. They would do better to use less virtuous talk and to act in a more honest way. I'll end on this point: it is best to be wary of our judgment of others. We can admire certain people for their obvious good qualities and thank God for having given them to us, but it is best to accept ourselves as we are. We may be aware that perhaps our own aptitudes are somewhat limited, but in our hearts we will be striving to develop them as best we can. It's in the little things that God intends to make us great.

CHAPTER 3

Is patience a virtue I should develop?

It's true that we are always in need of patience as the letter to the Hebrews reminds us. Remember how far Christ Himself went to be patient with us. This may have struck you when you see how passionate he was in his encounters with the women and men who crossed his path. He took as much time with noisy little children as he did with the elderly and the sick. He didn't get upset, either, when His apostles seemed particularly *"thick-headed"* in their understanding of him and his actions. But it was above all, in the ultimate sense of His own existence that He showed us just how far the virtue of patience could go. He, the Son of God, resolved that question once and for all. He did not cheat death. He never threatened anyone, even in His own legitimate self-defense. He went to the very end in His Passion...that kind of patience consists of something much more than keeping calm in a torrential rainstorm when the bus is running late.

I suggest that you not limit your patience to any particular area. If you did, you could leave yourself open to being taken over by an occurring situation and you would be helpless before it. You see, I know some people who intellectually accept the idea of noble suffering and showing patience in heroic situations. They assure their friends that they would risk their very lives for a humanitarian operation; they would allow themselves to be taken hostage in service of the truth; or again, they would be happy to suffer for their beliefs. Others take pleasure in showing their generosity through financial investments of an ethical nature. If these attitudes do not remain simply theoretical, then they are magnificent! But they do risk simply remaining pious intentions; above all, being subject to the temptation for glory and notoriety which such actions could bring in the sight of other people, as well as in the eyes of those who imagine they could carry them out.

True patience is not involved only with *"hypothetical"* situations. To subject oneself calmly to the malicious attacks of one's adversaries in a difficult situation offers a great opportunity to reveal your strength of character and self-control. To have problems with people whom everyone else holds in high esteem, to quarrel on occasion with your friends, to endure conflicts within your own family; this is where your patience can really be put to the test. I know a bishop who suffered very much from the criticism that a well-known and respected monk leveled at him. The unjust vicious gossip that was circulating freely all around him had absolutely no effect on him.

It's like this: the sting of a bee is more painful that that of a mosquito. The mistreatment we receive from people who we consider great, the negative things they express in our regard, are much more unbearable than the difficulties that ordinarily confront us. Believe me, it is far from rare that people who are reputed to be fair with their advice, and professional in their manner, can also sometimes get caught up in inconsistencies or misjudgments which do them much harm!

Be patient, not only in the great difficulties of life that confront you, but also in the consequences that follow on their heels. We are often willing to accept difficulties—just as long as they don't cause too much disruption in or lives, if you please! When we're young, we really would like to be patient when our father is at work when we'd rather have him home. But at the same time, we also would like to be able to give gifts to our friends and go on vacation with them—even if that really puts a strain on the family budget. Much later on, in a similar type of situation, we'd like to offer our own children everything that our more fortunate neighbors give theirs. We often want to adopt the same lifestyle they have.

It's the same way when it comes to sickness; we don't choose our illnesses, but being sick is no reason to be unbearable or disagreeable with everyone, especially those trying to help us!

My advice to you is to avoid or stop constantly moaning or complaining about the wrongs that have been done to you. Often we perceive the injustices that have been done to us as being much worse than they actually are. So, if you need to confide in someone, do not choose someone who loves to or has a tendency to get all upset and criticize others. Choose someone instead who is stable and has a steady demeanor. This kind of person will help you to reflect rationally on the problem at hand and have a calming influence. Otherwise, the person you confide in will not pull out the *"splinter"* that is causing your pain, but will push it more deeply into your wound intensifying that pain.

I know people who don't complain directly. However, they seek and find every means and opportunity possible to make others understand how much and in how many ways the miseries of the world are beating them down. In this way, they make it obvious to others just how patient and courageous they truly are. That's a good example of *"false patience."*

The truly patient person does not spend his or her time moaning and groaning about their problems. Confronted with them, they talk about them sincerely and with out exaggeration. If someone should pity them for something that isn't actually causing them to suffer—they have the simplicity to say so and call it like it is!

Experience will teach you that difficult situations, events or trying times can bring about something new. In a sense it's a kind of a *"giving birth."* When a mother is in labor—when she is giving birth—her physical suffering and pain is great. But she accepts it as part of her motherhood—she is giving birth to a new life, and this is truly a marvelous honor, and brings great joy as well! Therefore I encourage you to be courageous in the midst of life's difficulties and trials.

When you are sick, you experience suffering to a greater or lesser degree—mild or harsh. Intense suffering was something that Christ neither explained nor avoided. He confronted it as best he could.

During illness, treatments can be difficult. Sometimes we have to submit to them over and over again. We do this because we want to get well and live fully again. This desire to get well is actually a powerful motivating force which can sometimes, once we have recovered and matured from our experience, inspire and help us to live more deeply in the service of others and in our encounter with God. Sometimes we have to face the reality that a cure will not be part of our story, and we learn to value each moment as we await our ultimate face-to-face encounter with God.

Let's come back to my favorite subject—bees. They make honey with the very bitter juice of flowers. All we have to do is to bite into a flower to be convinced of this. Trials, difficulties, anguish and suffering, are bitter, yet they mold us in a certain sense, if we can recognize this, to be better people.

A last piece of advice for this chapter is to suggest that you seek an opportunity to approach this land of suffering. Don't close or cover your eyes. Don't run away. Our Church often presents us with Christ on the cross. He is almost naked, abandoned, denounced by his friends—rejected. His physical suffering is atrocious. We tend not to dwell too much on those things because we see the crucifix so often that it is very familiar to us. So what I am asking is that you become aware of, and embrace those who are suffering—those right around you. You may be able to give your time, your smile, or your availability to the sick, elderly, and those suffering in any way. This will not only be food for your spiritual and daily reflection, but a potentially life-altering experience. Look around—our world is not lacking in people who are suffering—believe me!

CHAPTER 4

Seeking Simplicity: doesn't this mean depriving myself of many things?

Over the years, I've learned that certain birds referred to as kestrels, know, in some mysterious way, how to frighten birds of prey and put them to flight. As a result, these episodes are much appreciated by gentler birds such as doves that like to be in their company. You'll notice that, in a similar way, simplicity can protect us against many difficulties. In a sense, simplicity put quite simply is an attitude or demeanor of *"detachment"* or *"unclutteredness"* that can keep us focused on what is truly important for life's journey. Also since this virtue contains a very pronounced Gospel flavor, it's not a bad idea to try it!

There are some occasions of pride that are quite delicate, such as having relatives in influential positions, belonging to a prominent and well known family, or owning the latest sports car or a powerful and popular motorcycle. I can't help thinking that, if there is any reason for pride in that, it shouldn't be attributed to the driver or the motorcyclist, but to the high quality of the machine itself.

Some people pay a lot of attention to their appearance, their hair, being stylishly dressed in the latest fashions and best brands, being a good dancer...others are exceedingly proud of their intellectual abilities, as though everyone should be impressed by their diplomas and degrees. Still others are very proud of their physique, their coordination and athletic ability, or their good looks or beauty, thinking that everyone should be wowed and bowled over by them. All these things, although they may well bring about a fleeting moment of understandable pride, are very transitory. They can change in an instant. It's a shame to put so much stock in them.

Consumer groups are always telling us that we really need to analyze the products we choose to buy. It's the same way when it comes to people. Before we can decide whether or not someone is gifted, wise, or generous, we need to decide whether he or she is of simple demeanor and has a good, honest and straightforward attitude toward life.

It is said that pearls that are formed during storms have only the outer shell...they are hollow. When pride forms the structure of a person's personality—the result is similar.

Don't put too much importance in popularity, celebrity or worldly honors. Beauty or honors that are not simple are not good. We become quite disagreeable when we are self-centered and become overly sensitive. If you are recognized for certain academic abilities, or for your talent and success in a sport, be happy for it—with simplicity. To noisily demand the recognition and praise of others for your achievements will make you appear quite selfish and many may not want to associate with you.

Here are some examples that may help you. The peacock, which shows all its beautiful feathers when it fans its tail, actually succeeds in displaying the part of its hind end anatomy that makes it least noble. Our mountain's most beautiful flowers wither very quickly once they are picked. You see that it is far more preferable to profit from your gifts and successes in all simplicity, rather than to draw attention to the fact that they are being recognized. Yet, you probably know some *"want to be"* people who are always seeking acclaim and recognition, as though this were all they had to do. Of course, I'm not talking about those who have an important job that requires some visibility and notoriety.

A comparison comes to my mind on this subject. When ships began to return from the New World, they brought back great quantities of gold, and they also brought monkeys and parakeets. The sailors brought them on board because it cost them practically nothing and because there was little risk of increasing the weight of the ship to any great degree. In my opinion, it's best to consider honors in this same way. Take on the gold of simplicity and add to it some small superficial satisfaction that will not occupy your mind too much. Having said this, you'll understand that there do exist certain situations where it is better to adopt the dress and behavior for which the occasion calls. For example it would be ridiculous to attend a formal reception in jogging shorts! Enough said!

CHAPTER 5

Some ongoing thoughts for those times of "storm warnings"

Curiously, it's not always the times of the greatest temptations that create the most damage to our spiritual lives. Fortunately, we are stronger than we often believe ourselves to be. Know that, if you are facing a time of interior tempest, God will deprive you neither of his presence, nor of His help.

When there's a serious accident, the victim is sometimes unconscious, and the rescuers may think at first that he or she died. One of the first things that they will do in such a case is to discern whether the heart is still beating. If it is, there's still a chance of reviving the person. Sometimes it happens that the violence of the temptations we face and experience seems to completely kill our willpower, and we are spiritually knocked out. We become spiritually unconscious. All that remains to discern is whether the heart is still beating, and that is most often the case. By that I mean that, in the deepest part of your being, your center or *"heart"* it is probable that you have not fully consented to what you are doing. As long as there is a reason to express your gratitude to your Creator. I'd like to emphasize this point a bit; think of all that has been given to you in coming into this world, and into your own unique life; think about the circumstances, events, and encounters that have molded you. Also consider the talents that you sometimes waste, the opportunities from which you neglect to profit in order to grow and advance in your life. When you compare what God has done for you and what you are doing for God and for others, how do you feel? Maybe it's quite simply what the gospel tells us of Mary when she cried out; *"My soul magnifies the Lord, who has done great things for me!"*

Now, on the contrary, it may be that you do not have this same spiritual disposition for another reason entirely. Perhaps you think that you are worthless, nothing, and completely lacking in talent. You may imagine that you're like garbage. But if people took you at your word and began to treat you that way, you certainly would be amazed! Often we tend to devalue ourselves; to *"put ourselves down,"* in order that people pay attention to us...how nice and reassuring it is to see ourselves the center of attention. *"What? Of course you're not worthless!"*

As the Gospel describes it, we pretend to be modest, and we take a seat at the far end of the table in order that someone will notice us and wave us up to the choicest seat. True simplicity doesn't play those kinds of games. It's not worth it to embarrass yourself by uttering a whole mumble jumble of humble words. True simplicity takes no notice of oneself at all.

Don't pretend to want to take the last place if it's not what you really want. It's important for me to clarify what I just said. We live in a society where being polite is considered a form of respect for others. To let someone go ahead of us in line, or to allow that person to serve himself first is not false simplicity. Similarly, to offer a compliment that is not entirely sincere in order to encourage someone is not necessarily hypocrisy. It is common practice to exaggerate our thinking a bit, but it's with the good intention of being kind and agreeable to others.

There are those who leave personal prayer or the encounter with God for the saints. They judge themselves either to be incapable of it, or to be unworthy of conversing with God. There are some others who refuse to go to Holy Communion, or who don't want to receive the sacrament of Confirmation because they believe that they're not pure enough. Still others refuse to use their talents in the service of God and others because they know they're just too miserable and weak, or that they would run the risk of being too proud by helping others. All that is nothing but a collection of poor fabrications and excuses. It's primarily a justification not to become involved.

"Ask for a sign from the Lord your God in the heavens or in the depths of the sea" says the prophet to King Ahaz in the book of Isaiah (Is 7:11). The king found himself in a very difficult situation at that moment, as rumors of war with another powerful kingdom were rampant. King Ahaz responded: *"No, I will not ask for a sign, and I will not put the Lord God to the test."*

That reaction displeased God, according to the text. It may have implied the king's humility and simplicity since he did not feel worthy to ask something of God. But the Lord decided to send him a sign anyway. The lesson of this passage is clear; when God wants to give you a gift, it would be a shame for you to disregard it. Your God gives you gifts and expects you to be able to put them to good use in all simplicity. To hide them or push them aside would be to show your ingratitude.

Actually, God wants just one thing for you; that you become the best you can be. God Himself is perfect and you are created in the image and likeness of God. God will help you to be your best. If you only rely on your own strength, you risk encountering many trials. But if you know your own limits and your own weaknesses, all the while putting all your hope in what God has given you, you will find strength and courage in that confidence. We must know how to be bold in all simplicity. Seek the advice of your spiritual director if need be but by all means forge ahead!

To imagine or think you know what you actually don't know is foolish. To pretend to be a specialist in an area in which you are not really strong or in which you are not trained presents a kind of vanity that will quickly make you unbearable to others. As for me, I would rather not present myself as a specialist, even in an area where I am strong. But I also would not want to pretend that I didn't know anything in that area; that would be ridiculous and disrespectful of myself and of others. When charity requires it, it's very good to be able to communicate with others and offer what may be useful to them. In fact, it is even better to do a little more than is asked of you. Your generosity in sharing your knowledge of a specific area in which you excel, will show good will and please others. Do not be afraid to show your own talents, if it is done in order to serve!

There are some very exotic trees that close their magnificent red flowers at sunset, and open them again to the rising sun. The people living where those trees are found tell the story that their trees go to sleep at night. Likewise, the simplicity that you are invited to live by following Christ allows you to place your talents and virtues to rest so you don't become overbearing, but also to awaken them in the service others in the sun of your availability.

It's wise that you avoid playing the sage just as much as playing the fool...you may have heard of certain people who may be recognized as mystics. They like to pass themselves off as being a little eccentric, or to seem less intelligent than they are in order to humiliate themselves before God. That's another example that it's better not to imitate. These mystics have judged it to be good to act that way in their very particular circumstances. There is an episode in the Bible where King David, who was so filled with joy to see the Ark of the Covenant enter his city of Jerusalem, that he did a frantic dance naked in the street. He was not trying to shock the spectators, but rather to somehow express through his extraordinary action the immense mystical connection and joy that he was feeling. He did this with extreme simplicity, with no thought to what others might think of him.

His wife reproached him when he was finished dancing, asking him if he might like to see a therapist. King David accepted her criticism with the greatest simplicity, quite satisfied to be the brunt of her reprimand, and thus be humiliated and humbled for his God. His former joy was so great however, that he hardly felt the sting of his humiliation. If your simplicity and your desire to follow Christ draw you criticism and sarcasm, I advise you to act like David. Don't allow these criticisms to sting or discourage you in the least, since the reason for them is not found in yourself, but in those who deliver the criticism.

CHAPTER 6

What can you do if you're super-conscious of your own limits?

Now, I'm going to go one step further and tell you that you should even appreciate your faults! Very simply, it's because it allows you to maintain a degree of simplicity, the same simplicity sung by Mary in the wonderful song of her *Magnificat*. *"The Lord has looked with Mercy on my lowliness...all ages will call me blessed."* (Lk. 1:48) By this, our Blessed Mother meant that her humility and her simplicity were so valuable to her Lord that they drew God to overwhelm her with graces and blessings. *"Humility"* is a beautiful word, don't you think? It comes from the Latin, *"humus"* which means *"earth,"* and indicates that you are in solidarity with everything that is of the earth; that you understand very well just who you are.

There is however, a very big difference between humility and disrespect for oneself. Humility is never a negative, self-deprecatory sentiment. You need to appreciate yourself as you are; that is true humility. It is also important to have a very positive and optimistic appreciation for those with whom you share this earthly journey.

In order to better understand what I'm going to say, you'll agree that, if you must confront trials and tribulations, some may appear ignoble or unjustified and others may appear noble and honorable. In many ways it is easier to accept suffering for something honorable without too much difficulty, but we don't accept it too easily when it is suffering for something that may be reprehensible. I hope a few examples may help.

I know some dedicated individuals who live in incredible poverty, and everyone respects and admires their immense simplicity. I know too that the really *"in"* thing for them to do is to share their meals that they put together from what didn't sell at the grocery store. We admire this but at the same time we are far from having the same esteem for the homeless person on the street corner who scavenges the garbage can or the guitar picker in the subway tunnel who doesn't smell very good! It's not so rare for us to experience inner feelings of contempt, or in any case, to believe that their situation is nothing really worthy of our notice or concern.

We can look at another example of this subject as something that may come from your youth. I suspect that you had a good *"talking to"* from your father for something silly that you did, and when the talk was over, everything returned to normal. In the moment you had no other choice but to accept that situation patiently, especially if it was justified. Now let's look at today. If you show that same kind of patience with a road rage driver who just insulted you because he thinks you just cut him off, and you decide not to become upset, you'll most likely be considered weak and a coward. This is what I mean by an *"ignoble"* or unjustified trial.

If someone has an abscess on his arm, and another on his face, the first will hurt, but the second will invite repulsion as well. He will have to suffer the indignity of watching everyone turn his eyes away with a look of revulsion.

Now, I need to tell you that you must not only accept the bad, which puts your patience to the test, but you must even love those difficulties because they will ultimately make you a more humble person.

Today, the virtue of patience is not appreciated very much. The same goes for the virtues of being understanding, simple or humble. The virtues of generosity and courage carry with them, much more prestige. If you want to follow the Gospel, though, I invite you to be generous toward others as well as to pardon those who have wronged and hurt you.

A generous heroic humanitarian action, or undergoing a selfless operation such as offering one's own kidney to someone in dire need would be perceived as wonderful works, and justly so. An act of forgiveness, however, or a desire for reconciliation on many levels, but especially with someone who has caused one hurt or loss of reputation would be considered as naive, a vain illusion, or just plain stupidity. A young man or woman who refuses to smoke, take part in some late night alcohol-driven activity, or some other more exploitive behavior risks being considered a pitiful *"goody two shoes"*, *"out of it"*, or a *"loser."* To accept personal responsibility and accountability for one's self in such situations, and to live with the criticism, rash judgment, and exclusion that may result from a true response to one's convictions, is to embrace the particular kind of difficulty that Jesus addresses in the Beatitudes.

Here's another situation that you may have faced. If you have ever had to take care of someone who is quite sick or suffers from a long-term illness or disabling condition, you realize that it is not easy. Some situations are just plain difficult and repulsive. However, when you gather yourself together and get beyond your fears, you will find an extraordinary satisfaction in helping those people. I would even say that you would know enormous fulfillment because you have gone beyond your own trials.

Even if we finally do come to accept and appreciate our trials, still, let's not be masochistic in any sense of the word. Evil is never good, in and of itself. Our God came to confront it. If I were to have a large wound or tumor on my face, I would have to practice great patience, humility, and courage, but above all I would have to do my best to be healed of it. If I had committed an indiscretion or an error in judgment that had no significant consequences, I would feel rather ashamed, and would thus practice a certain amount of simplicity. If this indiscretion had consequences affecting others, however, I obviously would have the duty to make reparation and redress the wrong that I've done...but keep in mind that it is also not a good choice to allow yourself to continuously look ridiculous in the eyes of others under the pretext of being simple or humble.

Can I tell you which are the best trials we may have to undergo? They are the ones that happen to us accidentally. It's useless to dream about martyrdom in a country that hasn't persecuted Christians for centuries! On the other hand, in your daily activities, your jobs, and your relations with others, there certainly will be some unforeseen difficulties that arise. The beautiful words of Psalm 83 will then become your own: *"It is better to remain on the threshold of the house of my God than to live in the tents of the wicked."*

In offering his life for us on the cross, Christ became an object of derision and shame. What I have shared with you just now are things that may be a bit difficult to hear, but you are sure to find peace of mind and heart if you put them into practice.

CHAPTER 7

Don't I risk appearing foolish if I practice the virtue of simplicity?

How can you remain *"simple"* when there is such great competition for being in first place in exams, athletic events, job promotions and other competitions? How can you be humble when your resumè or *"curriculum vitae"* is geared to highlight your successes? How can you show respect for others when they are your competitors, or when being interviewed by companies recruiting candidates for a job with the goal of only keeping the *"best"* ones?

Our society is founded upon excellence. The person who doesn't know how to *"promote himself"* has a very slim chance of succeeding. As a result, we have a contradiction. How can you reconcile the reality that exists in our society with the gospel simplicity that casts doubt upon your being able to make any kind of lasting impression?

This problem is actually nothing new! The Book of Wisdom in the bible cautions us to *"be wary of fame."* You need to have self-esteem, and to be aware of your own worth. That's a question of transparency and truth. For the rest, it's your gifts and talents and how you use them that will enable you to have a positive influence on our world.

There's nothing for you to be ashamed about. On the contrary, to refuse to display your own worth will mean you will have no chance to be able to act positively in a society where each one must be aware of his/her own value.

I see a person's reputation as somewhat like the leaves on the trees. You'd really have to be extremely hungry to eat them. The leaves are pretty, and more importantly; they protect the tree's fruit when it is still tender. Your own notoriety is like that; it is secondary, but nonetheless it is extremely useful since it comprises the exterior aspects of your life. In addition, your reputation will protect your good points as the leaves protect the fruit on trees.

Let me explain. Out of self-respect you wouldn't want anyone to say things about you that would hurt your reputation. As a result, you have to be careful how you conduct yourself, don't you? This practice of self-control can be very helpful in unguarded moments or during temptation.

Keep a guard over your virtues and put them into practice for they not only foster your growth, they will protect you and they are pleasing to God. They are like fruit which can become really delicious. However in order to guard your virtues well, it is not necessary for you to make jam out of them! Your reputation is a powerful agent for conservation, which, has the advantage of being natural and effective at the same time, in contrast to the many chemical products used today for the production and preservation of apples and other fruit,

Don't be so particular about your reputation, though, that you can't bear it to be scratched up, even just a little. Some of my friends are so timid that they run to the doctor over the slightest thing and load themselves up with all kinds of medicine. In the long run, these drugs do them more harm than good and completely alter their behavior!

Bear with little injuries, unkind remarks, and untruths from time to time. To get all upset about these things can, in certain cases, only confirm the thoughts of those who will think, "Where there's smoke, there must be a fire." There are some dogs that will only bite those who fear them. It is the same with remarks that may spread about you. If you are too afraid for your reputation, it could mean that you don't have enough confidence in yourself, unless you actually may have many dubious things for which you must blame yourself.

Certain little villages that are built of wood at the edge of streams are sometimes swept away by floods in springtime. Nothing of the sort happens for great buildings made of stone or concrete...unless, of course, there is some kind of major catastrophe. In a similar way, with a little self-control and a true desire to live according to the values, challenges, and precepts of the gospel, you can ignore the excesses of wagging tongues and being swept away by worry and concern. It would be a proof of weakness for you to become too preoccupied with them. In any case, don't waste time daydreaming about being well respected by everyone either. That's impossible—it's not going to happen! By trying to be like a chameleon, you'll end up dying of exhaustion, especially if you're sitting on a plaid blanket.

Your reputation is just the outer sign that advertises the virtues you carry within you. If you are suspected of hypocrisy because you live your faith and show interest in your religion; if you are suspected of cowardice because you've decided to remain calm and pardon others for what they've done to you, don't worry about that. Those who judge you in such a way are silly, afraid, and incapable themselves of that kind of courage. If people talk about you in an unkindly manner, that should in no way deter you from the choices you have made; always prefer the interior fruit you have made your own instead of the exterior leaves of the judgments others will make about you.

There are some people whose esteem is important to us, and others whose opinions don't matter so much at all. To tear out one's beard by the roots or follow a treatment that makes our hair fall out could cause many problems and make us a little depressed in the short run. But going to the hairdresser, barber, or to shave will usually give us a lift and more vitality in the long run. So even if your reputation is somewhat damaged, or even completely ruined by the tongues of detractors that are sometimes *"as sharp as razors"* as King David says in Psalm 51, try not to be upset; it will return more solid than before. On the other hand, if some bad actions or a penchant for vice justifiably rip out the roots of your reputation, it will be more difficult to restore.

In certain circumstances, you have to know how to end a conversation that is becoming stupid and illogical, a habit that is destructive, or a relationship that is leading to nowhere. This is important especially if any of these things is damaging your good reputation. On the other hand, if you are being criticized for the choices you are making as a result of your desire to live the gospel, let the dogs howl at the moon; they will not be able to harm you in any way. The razor of their slanderous words will only enhance the elegant cut of your reputation.

Fix your thoughts once again on Christ. If He has warned us that sometimes we will be criticized and misunderstood, he has also shown us the road to happiness in the Beatitudes. In the end truth is always stronger than slander, though we must sometimes be quite patient in order to see it win out. One point has always struck me; Christ never wished to threaten anyone, whether it is a question of an arrest, as sneaky as it was lamentable, or a *"fixed"* trial and an execution that was as sordid as it was thorough. He took upon himself all the sufferings and humiliation of people who are unjustly treated, transforming all into victory by his resurrection.

What I'm telling you here requires, however, that you consider the possibility of exceptional circumstances. Never permit anyone to say very serious, unjust things about you. In that case, you must defend yourself very clearly; it's a question of self-respect and of loyalty to those who esteem you and have confidence in you. In that case, don't hesitate to show firmness and great courage.

CHAPTER 8

How can you maintain good self-control?

If you have been confirmed, you probably already know that the oil used by the bishop, the Holy Chrism, is made up of olive oil and balm. This combination represents the idea that, as the oil of faith is absorbed into your being, you are invited to breathe forth the lovely scent of the balm as a witness to others of that faith which, though hidden, is alive within you. I like the idea that the balm, which penetrates the skin in this mixture, is a symbol of simplicity, and the olive oil, which remains on its surface, symbolizes the kindness, which our Faith invites us to show others.

It is important that simplicity and kindness both live in our hearts. Don't allow yourself to be one of those people who only pay these virtues lip service allowing them to remain only theoretical. Also don't be like those who have convinced themselves that they are already simple, humble and kind, although they will often show the opposite by getting upset at the least little obstacle that gets in their way. There is a medicine called *"Oil of St. Paul"* which is used as an antidote for snakebites. It refers to a snake-bite, which did absolutely no harm to St. Paul at the time of his shipwreck; this incident is recounted in the Acts of the Apostles (28:1-6) in the bible. It is said that this serum is only effective if it is pure. I can see here a good comparison between that antidote and the simplicity that effectively combats the swelling of anger that contradictions and insults can cause in our hearts. If an insulting word, or an unjust judgment bites you, and if your temperament and nature tends to be more or less hot, you can become upset and even furious. You will then know that simplicity and self-mastery or control, are not deeply anchored within you, and that they remain only superficial.

You may remember the beautiful bible story about Joseph, one of the sons of Jacob who was sold into slavery by his brothers who unfortunately were jealous of his successes (Genesis 37-45). The text presents many different episodes as it relates this story. At the end of the tale, after many years, Joseph comes face to face with his brothers again in Egypt, and we see that he now finds himself in a situation of having extraordinary power. As a high-ranking Egyptian official, Joseph is confronting half starved Bedouins, who have come to negotiate the best price for much-needed food staples. Joseph has at his disposal all the power of the local police; his brothers are foreigners who can easily be suspected of any number of bad intentions. In that situation, Joseph could easily have used all the power he had at hand to enact great vengeance on his brothers for their past wrongs to him. However, as the story tells us, not only did he refuse to give in to vengeance, but on the contrary, he maintained perfect control over his anger. When allowing his brothers to leave for home, Joseph even gave them this ironic advice: *"Above all, do not argue along the way."* That story is one of the most beautiful parables of forgiveness that I have ever heard.

Our life on earth is a journey. Let's not then argue with one another along the way, but let's walk along as harmoniously as possible with the companions that are given to us. As far as anger goes, the best way to cope with it is to recognize and acknowledge it, but not to give into it at all. In this way, we will not give hatred an opportunity to enter into us.

It's true that sometimes we need to correct the faults of those who are confided to our care, especially if they are young, or if they are our own brothers and sisters. I advise you to do it gently but firmly, frankly, and without weakness, but at the same time with kindness and simplicity. It's been said that nothing calms the fury of an elephant better than the sight of a little lamb.

It's good to remember that, when we ourselves receive a correction that is made in anger, we often close our ears, and don't hear any more of what's being said. This kind of situation seems detestable to us. On the other hand, when correction is carried out in a peaceful discussion that appeals to our reason, we can admit the wrong and accept the consequences. This can have a much better effect on the outcome as we deal with restitution.

When a country is suffering from civil unrest, a forced appeasement dictated at the point of a gun will never be effective. It will only pave the way for further violence and a harsh revolt in the future. When force is used, there are always unforeseen consequences, even in the most highly disciplined armies. It's always better to use reason rather than anger, especially if the remarks to be made are well justified.

Now you might be thinking that in certain circumstances, you may have legitimate reason for getting angry, but this is flawed thinking. Once you have allowed hatred to take hold within you, even for a justifiable reason, you will not be able to get rid of it very easily. It starts out as only a tiny shoot, but hatred can quickly grow to be a large and aggressive invasive plant. The advice of the apostle is excellent: *"Do not let the sun go down on your anger."* At night, your anger may well turn into hatred, and I've never known an angry hate-filled person to believe that their anger and hatred was unjustified!

Learn to live without anger, rather than to think that you can master it to impress others. The first step is to recognize it and acknowledge it. In moments of fatigue or weakness, it risks erupting and surprising you. If that should happen to you, try to reject it quickly and channel the energy in another direction rather than to attempt to wrestle with it. Anger is like a snake; if it can get its head through an opening, then its whole body can quickly follow.

You're probably thinking that it's easy enough to say this...but how do we reject or deal with our anger? My advice from my own experience is to summon all your energy when you feel and recognize anger growing within you; not harshly, but seriously and with serenity. Don't be like the noisy school supervisors who, while yelling *"Silence!"* add more noise to the general state of confusion. By trying to control or suppress yourself too harshly, your anger might eventually erupt with even greater force and you could totally lose your self-control. Recognition is the first force of defense in dealing with this human reality.

St. Augustine had the chance to give this advice to a young bishop, *"Do what a man must do, and if anger gets the better of you, stop a moment and turn your thoughts directly to God."* An interior life that is open and allows for regular encounters with God will allow you to grow in spiritual depth and self-control. Act without delay. The best way to act when we have allowed ourselves to be trapped into lying is to reassert the truth immediately by admitting our straying from it. If anger gets the best of you, summon a smile, and make amends for your anger right away by displaying a better-controlled attitude. If you must, talk it out with someone who is neutral. We must not wait for the wound to become infected before treating it!

When you are fortunate enough to have a period of time when nothing comes along to test your nerves, be aware of this, and store up and set aside a good measure of calm and flexibility by being very attentive to the quality of your relationships with others.

CHAPTER 9

How can you accept yourself as you are?

It is extremely useful to cultivate the virtue of patience with yourself. It's useless to become angry over what you are, or to be miserable and despair over your imperfections. That would be the best way I know to make yourself even more unpleasant than you already may have been.

I know some people who are always getting angry because they have become angry, who despair over their misery and despair, or who are very sad because they became sad over what they are. They go from despair to resentment, a little like those frequent summer storms that eventually unsettle the entire season's weather...a preliminary burst of anger becomes an overture for a second burst which then prepares the way for the third, and so on. It's best to avoid this kind of syndrome. Often, you see, this kind of reaction finds its source in a prideful, self-love that is dismal when it realizes its own faults and imperfections.

It's true that our faults won't be pleasing to us, but it is best that this displeasure be tranquil, calm and firm.

You'll agree that a judge will pronounce a much more just sentence when he acts in a reasonable and calm manner, whereas if he judges his cases with impetuosity and passion, he won't be passing sentence on the deeds of the accused for what they are, but for what standards he sets for himself. We correct ourselves much better by expressing our regrets peacefully and calmly rather than by becoming moody and taking our anger out on ourselves.

These emotional reactions of ours are not usually equal to the seriousness of our faults, but instead, they often reflect the mood of the moment. For example, someone who wants and likes to remain pure, will become humiliated and furious, upset and disappointed with himself because he allowed himself to slip into looking at a movie, or some video on the Web that is a bit *"hard core"* or more. On the other hand, it may not disturb him a bit to have spread vicious, unfounded rumors that are ruining the reputation of one of his acquaintances. There are many more examples I could give of this kind of judgment which stems not from reason but from negative passions.

Believe me, a father's corrections have a much more positive effect on his child when they come from the heart rather than when they are being influenced by his uncontrolled anger. In the same way, you'll see that the patience which you exercise on your own behalf will be much more effective if it is accompanied by a real desire to change, and will accomplish more than tempestuous moods and rages ever will.

I can well imagine that if I were to become aware of my overbearing attitude toward others, I would say to myself, *"Francis, you are horrible, you are pathetic, and incapable of controlling yourself, since after all the many good resolutions you've made, you're really just a pitiful fellow. You should just die of shame! You are not even worthy to speak to this God to whom you owe everything, and whom you've so horribly deceived!"* I could go on and on with that silly, masochistic logic. However, in my opinion, it would be much healthier for me to say to myself, *"Well, it looks like I've fallen once again into an old fault that I had really wanted to correct...It's time to take hold of myself, and do better in the future. After all, it's not the end of the world for me to fall, but it would be much worse if I stayed on the ground. I'm going to ask God to help me by granting me increased humility, and at the same time, I'll pay really close attention to my attitude today."*

Now I'd like to look at ways that I can use my personality and correct myself, so that I'll be more successful at resisting the old faults that I know I possess. And as for the rest, it would be a good idea to talk it over with my spiritual director.

I hope you see that it serves no purpose for you to be too harsh with yourself. Even if you think that the *"soft"* method that I'm suggesting isn't sufficient to encourage you to repent, at least end your encounter with God by a prayer of confidence, as Psalm 42 suggests: *"Why are you downcast, Oh my soul, why do you groan within me? Hope in God, I will praise you still, my Savior and my God."*

Pick yourself up when you fall, and don't be too shocked at the fall. It's not surprising that a sick person should be handicapped, that weakness should be weak, and that you, a human being, should be fragile. Have infinite confidence in this God who wants you to be courageous and get on your feet in order for you to get back on the road to holiness!

CHAPTER 10

Can you work without panicking and live serenely and calm?

You are invited to bring *"care"* to your work which has nothing to do with panic or preoccupation. Be at peace. This doesn't mean that you should be indifferent to what you have to do which would be completely ridiculous...be aware that your work is a contribution to the creative act of God, and that you have something to do on this earth. This shouldn't cause you anxiety, but rather satisfaction and happiness. Don't panic, then. The Lord spoke of this to Martha in the Gospel according to Luke in Chapter 10. Martha you may remember, was panicking a bit over the cares of her home. The Lord did not reproach her at all for applying herself to her work, certainly, but rather for the kind of frenzy that prevents us from doing things well.

Those great rivers that flow tranquilly and allow for smooth sailing, contrary to other chaotic torrents of water that tear up everything during their flood stages and are not at all suited to navigation, always impress me. The rains from big storms are also very impressive, but they come fast and run off the surface of the dry land rather than soaking in, thus they don't quench the soil to any great degree. In our work, we must *"hurry slowly."* It's a question of respect for the task to be accomplished. When you do something well, the delays incurred are seen to fade in their importance.

Flies don't bother us because of what they are, but because of their buzzing. And it's true that any little worries can upset us in a similar way. Try to be organized and prioritize your duties but also accept serenely what life brings to you. You can't accomplish anything in one fell swoop, and if you try to do that, you'll simply give the impression of being overwhelmed and overcome by the events of your life.

In order to succeed, I advise you to do two things: have confidence in God who has put many talents and resources within you, while at the same time doing your own part well. In this way you will work on the one hand as if your success depends only on God, in whom you put all your confidence and on the other hand as if it all depends on the effort and resources that you yourself give to the work.

This reminds me of an observation that has always amused me about little children when they are hiking in the mountains. They hold onto their father's one hand, and with the other they pick strawberries in the woods. Remain a little childlike, like that. While you are juggling all your duties with one hand, remember to also hold onto the hand of your Heavenly Father. Return to him from time to time, as the little children do to see if he approves of what you are doing...don't let go of His hand, thinking that you'll be able to accomplish more, because if you abandon Him, you risk falling flat on your face.

More specifically, this means that when you are in the middle of some work that doesn't demand all of your attention, you can turn your thoughts toward God. If your work does demand more concentration, those thoughts will have to be more fleeting. You'll then be like the sailors who steer by the stars in order to reach the point of land they're aiming for. In this way, God will be at the heart of your work, with you and in you and will give much deeper meaning to it.

CHAPTER 11

Obedience?

You probably know that, in our Church, those in religious or consecrated life take vows to live the rest of their lives in poverty, chastity and obedience. It's a very beautiful promise, which I won't go into in depth here since you are probably not in religious life. The objective of these vows is, in any case, to live intensely the evangelical or gospel counsels and challenges of the Beatitudes. It's not necessary to make such a promise, though, in order for you to profit from this dynamic, since everyone is invited by the Lord to live these Gospel Counsels each in his own way.

Experience has no doubt shown you that you obey either out of necessity or by choice. First, you do so by necessity, because, in one way or another, you are part of an hierarchy, whether as part of a school or at work. The rules you receive may or may not be acceptable to you. In the first case, I suppose there would be very few problems. However, in the second case you need a lot of humility and patience to accept rules that make sense, but with which you don't agree.

What is much more beautiful is that you can choose freely to obey. If it is true that we cannot usually choose our parents or teachers, and often our bosses or their supervisors either, you can choose your spiritual director. You can also decide to make a promise to a particular association, organization, or take part in an activity that will be under the authority of a responsible person. You will then be obeying the by-laws of the organization or the directives of a leader, and various objectives stemming from these situations that give a certain order, sense and shape to your life. You'll be putting yourself voluntarily at the service of another person or a cause.

Fidelity to your promise will be very important, because you'll know that people will be counting on you. It is a beautiful thing to accept the idea that your sense of freedom can be enriched in this way and not just by following your own feelings, wants and desires. If you accept the idea of making yourself available for service, you'll be sure to be there when you're needed and you'll find a dynamism there that will truly contain the flavor of the Gospel.

CHAPTER 12

What is purity?

Purity is a word or concept that may not be too popular these days, but it's still a beautiful thing. You may be thinking *"It's not easy."* I invite you not to compromise on this point in your day-to-day life. To remain pure means maintaining a courageous attitude that does not give in easily, and a respect for your own dignity and that of others. Keep watch over your imagination; it will be tested often. Know too that it is much more difficult to climb back up the hill than to refuse a questionable invitation.

When a fruit is spoiled, you can try to salvage it or to use it to make a pie or pastry. But it's still harder to do then than when the fruit remains fresh. Don't make the excuse that exploring questionable television channels or Internet sites is just a means of expressing your blossoming sexuality. Prepare yourself for later on. That way, when you meet someone who will inspire you to say, *"I love you,"* you'll be able to tell him or her of your long struggle and to say in all honesty, *"I have been waiting for you, and you alone."*

Many a TV series shows you the delicious, tantalizing and pleasing aspects of the games of love and chance. It would be a great shame to take these fictitious shows at face value. Don't be like the butterfly that, attracted by the beauty of the fire, and thinking it is as harmless as it is beautiful, burns its wings. There are some delights that completely lose their appeal in the clear light of a new day.

In marriage as well, self control, and a good mastery of your sensual appetite will be necessary. Illness and any number of life's trials and situations can challenge you to endure periods of chastity which your life as a Christian will invite you to live in fidelity to your spouse and your God.

CHAPTER 13

A little advice on this subject

Be careful not to give into a *"wishy-washy"* or an *"it doesn't matter"* or an *"it's not going to hurt anybody"* attitude. Often things start out slowly, but the downhill speed picks up rapidly. In this area it would be better to refuse initially than to try to fix a bad situation later on.

<u>We are fragile beings</u>. Everything in nature is corruptible. Even the clearest water becomes polluted when flies fall into it and drown. To experiment a little when you think you can control the situation is not without danger. Purity is a question of self-respect, a question of the heart, whereas impurity leaves out the heart and is a disrespect of the senses that makes oneself or another an object of gratification.

You will never see bees gathering nectar from road-kill, dead animals! On the contrary; they flee from the stench that emanates from it. The best thing to do is to imitate them.

The magnificent text that sings of love in the Bible, the Song of Songs, exalts a pure, sincere and lasting love. The portrait of young people in love in this text is equally beautiful from a physical and moral point of view.

If you recognize that others somewhat easily influence you, be very careful about the company you keep. Certain people are dangerous, and they take pleasure in initiating others into the questionable ways with which they have already done some experimentation themselves.

Have courage in this area too; Christ is a demanding Friend, who will speak to you more often of the beauty of the mountain summits than of the fog of the valleys.

CHAPTER 14

How can you be poor while maintaining a standing in the world that is not truly poor?

"Happy are the poor; the Kingdom of Heaven is theirs." If you interpret this Beatitude literally, you can immediately deduce, as the Gospel text tells us shortly after the above quotation, that *"unhappy are the rich."* Who is this text actually speaking to? The rich to whom this Beatitude refers are not so much those who possess riches of intelligence and talents, but those who use all their intelligence and talents in the pursuit and preservation of their wealth. Above all, it has to do with a person's attitude and will!

I've heard of a water bird called a kingfisher that makes its nest in a very unusual way. It builds a floating, spherical nest with a small opening that points toward the sky. This nest is never submerged, since it is constructed to resist the worst floods and storms. Your heart can be like these water nests, opening upward, that is to say, toward heaven, impenetrable against temptations to wealth and worldliness, but nonetheless floating perfectly amidst a world tainted by money, having to have the right brand,

and all sorts of other material distractions. Don't allow yourself to be seduced, fascinated or overwhelmed by the false promises of money, power, and success.

In some work places, the employees there regularly use extremely toxic products without being harmed, especially if they take specific precautions while using them. These precautions allow the employees to keep those products in their proper place and usage rather than letting them be absorbed into their own veins. You can live in a world tainted by riches without being contaminated by them yourself, as long as your bank account remains in the bank and is not deposited in the vault of your heart. If money is not everything to you, you'll be able to live in great interior freedom, and you will find the road to happiness that sharing with others offers.

Try to be generous. No one likes to hear the term "*egotist*" applied to himself. No, it is much more common to hear someone excuse himself as being unable to help others financially because he has children to take care of, or because he needs to put money aside for education or emergencies, or because after all, he is not exactly wealthy. Avarice or greed is thus a serious illness since it is never diagnosed by the one affected by it, who is acting in all good conscience.

In the book of Exodus 3:1ff, Moses remained transfixed before the burning bush, which burned without being consumed. I like to see in this episode a beautiful example of charitable giving; if you act with generosity, you will not be consumed, you will not be destroyed; on the contrary, you will be illuminated and enlightened! Avarice, however, is the exact opposite of this. It is also a kind of fire, but one that consumes the entire person and gives him a terrible fever, which he mistakes for a very natural and agreeable desire.

Believe me, if you spend your time wishing for things you don't have, you are wasting your time. If you are very much attached to your possessions, being fixated on them such that you think about them often and are in agony at the idea of losing them, there too, you are inflicting upon yourself a kind of fever that is not at all healthy.

In summary, it's not useful to wish for things that you don't have, and it's not necessary to be too attached to what you do have.

CHAPTER 15

How can you practice the Gospel counsel of poverty while remaining part of your society?

I know some people with some very complex personalities. They are courteous and extremely annoying, simple and yet proud, timid, but very outspoken. That has already been said of the people of Athens, who in ancient times were known for the variety and versatility of their characters. I would like to propose to you here the paradox of living with a certain amount of consumerism, while at the same time following the Gospel counsel of poverty. I would like you to be able to conduct your duties and affairs with responsibility, attention and the care required, while at the same time *"despising money,"* as the gospel advises.

A preliminary point in order to reassure your parents, those close to you, and your banker; you should apply yourself to managing your investments well and skill-fully drawing profit from them, and even more so, if it's possible, in the case of those for whom making a profit is their primary field of specialization.

I have always been impressed by the work of those municipal gardeners who put such extraordinary care into the work of maintaining and developing the green areas of the city, even though the properties they work on don't belong to them personally. Why do they do this? Undoubtedly, it's done out of professional pride, but also out of the personal pride they take in making these areas pleasing to all citizens of the city.

God has given us this earth so that we can make of it a beautiful garden. It's not for love of ourselves that we labor, but for a mission that goes beyond ourselves. Participating in the creative action of our God is not a difficult chore for us; rather, there is a positive goal toward which we are aiming, and this motivates us to do our best. I advise you to do your work in the most careful and efficient way possible, taking care not to be tempted by feelings of personal ownership of it. Be especially vigilant not to confuse your own interests with those of God! In order not to make a mistake here, I suggest that while carrying out your work, you practice poverty of spirit.

"Poverty of spirit," you may be wondering...are these just empty words that might just create an alibi for my conscience? It would be a shame to see things in this way. Rather, it's a disposition or attitude of spirit that must translate into concrete actions. Very practically speaking, I suggest that you find a way to share yourself, your gifts and goods, with those who have less than you do. It's a good exercise in divesting yourself of an over accumulation and overabundance of goods, and there is no shortage of

organizations that are looking for donations as well as for participants to volunteer their time in furthering their good works.

You can even do much more, by approaching people in difficult circumstances, giving them a little of your time, your talent, and your availability. This is how you can become aware of a wider world that would otherwise remain unknown to you. We no longer see things the same way once we have had the opportunity to meet some people who are in precarious financial and economic situations.

Would you like to do even more? Make yourself even poorer than the poor. How? By putting yourself at the service of the poor. While you are with them, make them your masters. Put yourself at the service of the sick in the most concrete way possible. For example, run errands for the elderly; cook for them, clean their homes, maybe even help with their grooming. Do this with your own hands, and not by hiring someone else to do it. It's a royal gift to serve the Lord by serving the most humble among us.

In centuries past, St. Louis, the King of France completely amazed his entourage by giving them this kind of example. Today, many people, from the simplest employee to the wealthiest employer, give their time and availability on a regular basis to places where there are those in need, such as a homeless shelter or a local soup kitchen.

The Beatitudes remind us in a very direct way, *"Blessed are the poor, for the Kingdom of Heaven is theirs. I was hungry, and you gave me to eat; I was cold and naked, and you clothed me; now enter into the Kingdom prepared for you from the foundation of the world."* This is what the King of Kings who is King of the poor will say on the great Day of Judgment, according to the fifth chapter of St. Matthew's Gospel (cf. Mt. 5:1 and 25:31-46).

There's another way of living this spirit of poverty and simplicity, simply by being aware of and using the events that happen in your life. Don't neglect to profit from these moments that give you an opportunity to have less, to live under difficult conditions, or to do something without your usual creature comforts: going camping with few *"extras;"* facing difficult weather conditions; participating in a humanitarian service opportunity. These are all open doors for you to rediscover the nomadic roots of our faith. Seek out and embrace these types of challenging situations freely and good heartedly, as experiences that will make you love poverty.

There's also the possibility of having to face unforeseen events that can make you unexpectedly poorer if you are, for example, the victim of a burglary, a fire, or an accident of some sort. By being able to face these unfortunate surprises with calm and patience, you'll know that you are making progress in the spirit of poverty. Don't complain about your problems! Our goods are not, as in the case of animals, fur coats that cannot easily be removed, but rather like our clothing that can be changed or discarded (even quickly) if need be.

CHAPTER 16

How can you be rich in spirit while being materially poor?

I would not like you to think, as you read this, that I'm only addressing young people from affluent backgrounds in this book. If you are among the materially poor, you are surely living at a level of simplicity that you have hardly chosen for yourself. In this case, it would be helpful to remind yourself that the Lord did not live in privileged circumstances in His time either.

If you are living in a degree of poverty, you have already run part of the road that leads toward true simplicity. You have discovered this path quite naturally because of your circumstances, whereas others will have much more difficulty finding it!

Here is an important point; accept yourself as you are, and your present situation as well. The Lord has undoubtedly given you many riches other than those that can be seen or experienced through any level of consumerism or accumulation even in your own family.

Another point is to remind you that you really are *"living simplicity."* Some people take vows of poverty to do this, but you are actually living it. You didn't choose it and yet you are living what is so much admired in others.

Don't be afflicted or conflicted by the state of your poverty. Do not be ashamed of it. God himself became a beggar for our love. By being poor, you will understand much more easily the difficulties experienced by those who surround you in this world, and you will know that true wealth is found elsewhere than in material goods.

CHAPTER 17

Who are your friends?

The most important point in your existence is to love. This sentiment, which is at the heart of life, is recalled throughout all of the pages of the Gospel. Yet we see how differently people will interpret the meaning of this word!

The problem is that this very, *"to love,"* is used to speak about chocolate, computers, cars, music, food, one's friends, one's spouse or one's country... and we'd better not love our friends in the same way we love our chocolate!

This wonderful word can still be quite formidable in certain circumstances. Loving something that is really evil can make you run the risk of turning everything that is important in your life evil as well. The young Nazis in 1936 who sincerely loved their party, and were so enthusiastic about their demonstrations, became veritable monsters of human beings and we know what happened.

Since friendship is justly considered one of the strongest sentiments of our existence, it can be extremely beneficial when it permits us to profit from the virtues of our friends. Let's be wary that it never brings out the worst, but always the best in others and us.

In friendship, good communication is essential. I'll come back to that in a moment. The honey of the mountains is better than many other kinds because the bees have gathered their nectar from flowers of extremely high quality. On the other hand, there is a type of honey that is actually poisonous; it makes those who consume it insane because the bees have gathered nectar from poisonous flowers. In like manner, friendship that is founded upon the sharing of evil things can also be extremely poisonous. If there exists, however an astonishing complicity among people to be able to do evil, there also exists an extraordinary capacity for sharing that permits people to work together in search of a shared ideal.

So, in order to live that beautiful reality of friendship, don't judge people by their outward appearances alone. Certain people are attractive because of their beautiful voice, face, physical ability or some other pleasing trait. Often, especially when we are young, we are most impressed by these outward qualities of people. We judge that a certain young man has many good qualities and traits and we become attracted and very excited about him. He dances so well, he's a fantastic surfer, he's well dressed, great at sports, very popular with his female friends and treats them well, and he has a first-class physique. These elements are certainly very appealing, but nothing stops the person who fits this overblown description from being a deceitful imposter or phony in all reality. It's not really right or healthy to want to base your friendship on such superficial traits, very simply because what makes up this kind of charm is like snow that melts in the sun. True beauty and the true person are more interior.

CHAPTER 18

What about flirting?

Most television shows for adolescents and young adults depict love as a fickle sport or game with many ups and downs played between young people. The clever casting technique of these shows make the participants seem as beautiful as they are carefree. Do you think that life is really so simple? You needn't turn on your TV in order to see couples blossoming with the springtime. In fact, now it seems to be springtime all year round!

Every feeling of being in love demands a great investment of your affection. Undeniably, there is great pleasure in that. Love itself is as old as humanity, yet its motives can sometimes be very changeable or even unreliable. They can be founded on a certain romanticism in search for that one special person. How do you know if you have found the right one?

There's a common and popular idea that everyone has a *"soul mate"* waiting for him or her somewhere, a sort of twin to oneself; someone about whom you'll be able to say, *"We're made for each other,"* like the key for the lock. This is a wonderful concept, but it is actually based on an illusion. The ideal partner, in and of himself or herself, simply does not exist. Lasting love takes continuous effort to adjust oneself to the other day by day each day.

I must say as well that there sometimes exists a kind of need to prove oneself to one's friends as capable of dating someone. Society urges each of us to show that we are *"sexually correct"* in maintaining a liberal, freethinking approach, which is supposed to help us to avoid frustrations. This now has come to the point where, today, words like *"virginity"* and *"chastity"* can seem obscene and ridiculous and abnormal to many. Most of the time these games of love, especially if they were begun at an early age, are not lasting and end in painful ruptures. I'm not denying the sincerity of the feelings of even very young people; the desire to love and to be loved is strong, and the passion of youth can produce intense feelings of *"love at first sight,"* and foster other tender moments. Some too, need to reassure themselves that they are capable of inspiring amorous sentiments in others. Others are very flattered to be able to date someone who is considered to be someone very attractive.

The majority of these adventures doesn't result in anything lasting and can sometimes be very damaging. That's why it's always rather unfortunate to have experienced or exploited those moments in a rush when they could have been lived very differently and in a more positive way. By this I mean to say that youth can also be a time that is particularly suited to forming broader friendships and to the possibility of discovering so many things other than the one single personality of that momentary partner. That is what, among other things makes that rushed exclusive experience unfortunate. Often built on rocky, but not very rational soil, these vain kinds of *"puppy love"* can sometimes leave a bitter taste. They can have painful consequences in our lives, leading to very little pleasure or affirmation, and leave within us great turmoil and consternation. Sometimes we live these relationships out as a kind of contest, in which we take part in actions that are not very responsible.

I imagine that one would hardly feel much pity for a snake charmer who is bitten by one of his serpents! It seems that there are also some spectators with morbid tastes who go to the circus hoping to see the lion tamer eaten by one of his lions. Do you think that someone can play with love without any consequences? Can he control it at will? He risks being badly bitten and then laughed at because, in desiring to tame love, he was surprised to find its bite was poisonous.

Let me assure you that my objective here is not to make a desert hermit out of you by crying out that all encounters between boys and girls are sinful! But it would trouble me if you thought that love was a game without any consequences, and that you could play on the keyboard, court, or field of love in a very casual manner.

Love is a magnificent thing. We must find ways to increase it in order to love God, in order to love others, in order to also love the person whom you may form a wonderful relationship that can develop into a lasting life together as a married couple. You must also store it up in order to love yourself as well. It's a shame to waste love.

One day you will be called to give an account of what you have done with your life, with your capacity to love, and with the time that was given to you. You will not do this before a demanding judge who seeks to condemn you, but before an infinitely loving father who desires your happiness, and that of others as well.

Where I come from, we say that it's not a good idea to plant a walnut tree in the middle of a vineyard. That tree exhausts the ground around it, because it grows to be huge. It also casts a great shadow over the vines, and you know how dense the shadow of a great tree can be. It's the same kind of thing with these games of love. They end up exhausting you and casting a shadow over all the rest of your life. So even if it's *the thing to do*, and even if everyone seems to be playing this game, I invite you to live this wonderful dimension of you existence in a way that is clear, true, and responsible.

CHAPTER 19

What is your opinion on friendship?

Today, friendship is usually considered to be a more restrained form of love. What would become of us if all our relationships were either exclusively amorous or simply functional? Certainly, the ideal would be to be able to maintain cordial relations with everyone. But it's also helpful to develop good relationships with those who can provide you with more than simple cordiality. Friendship is not born solely of a harmony of personalities, but from a mutual esteem and trust. It can arise from simple acquaintanceship or be founded upon intellectual compatibility, and can become a wonderful and fulfilling area of mutual sharing in your life, bound by fidelity and withstanding the test of time.

Your friendship will be even more meaningful if you and your friend can share what is most essential, the depth of your spiritual lives. It will be a most precious gift from God and will bring both of you closer to God. It will be made up of words and silences; it will become ever more fresh and renewed. This world is made for love, you know;

we must love it as we love our God. Friendship gives a foretaste of the harmony, and the achievement of the goal of relationship and sharing that is promised to us in the transfiguration to come in eternity.

You'll have understood that I am not speaking here of that kindness and understanding that we must try to have toward everyone in *"loving our neighbor."* Here I'm speaking about spiritual friendship, the possibility of sharing the road of faith with our companions on the journey. This sharing grows out of mutual respect and concern. It is not rigidly structured, or based upon obligations, but finds happiness in each encounter. Its advantages are many; it gives us the opportunity to confide in our friend; it will allow us to gain back our confidence when we go through trials, it can help us to overcome discouragement, and to more clearly analyze our problems. It can enlarge our horizons, suggesting to us new possibilities, and bring us new resources. Psalm 133 says these things beautifully: *"How good and how pleasant it is to live together as brothers and sisters together."*

Some people may tell you that this sentiment does not exist, or that it's a waste of time. How wrong they are! In the case of large monasteries, each monk must treat the other without any partiality, since the goal of each is to achieve true devotion to God in the stable environment of religious or consecrated life. However, let us who are in the world and not in the monasteries leave the monks on this point. Didn't the Lord himself have one apostle, John, for whom he felt a stronger friendship than for the other eleven? When the road up the mountain is slippery and perilous, it's extremely wise to hold onto one another with ropes. We need the rope of solid, healthy, and durable friendships in order to live in this changeable world, and to grow and make progress on the steep road to become all that God has created us to be.

CHAPTER 20

Be careful not to be naïve!

Just because you're a Christian doesn't mean that you should allow yourself to be taken for a fool! There's hardly any difference, from what I hear, between poisonous honey and the good honey from our mountains. If you were to mix them together, you wouldn't see anything unusual, yet everything would have been poisoned!

Be careful, because the attraction of this beautiful sentiment of friendship can, of itself, serve as a trap. It is better for you not to be naïve about it, and not to let yourself be fooled by anyone acting under the guise of friendship. Some people can seek to gain your confidence in order to use your good will in an unhealthy way.

I don't like anyone to be too naïve, and I advise you to be astute enough to be able to spot someone who is seeking to use the positive sentiments of others to his own advantage. These people are often very clever, and are good talkers, but once they no longer have any use for their targets, they quickly drop them. This is nothing like the frankness and simplicity of real friendship, which I have described to you previously. This false friendship, like our poisonous honey, provokes a kind of dizziness that makes its prey unsteady, and pushes him to engage in behavior that is not common to him. A true friend is more demanding, often because his objective is not to flatter someone in order to be able to manipulate him. Also, this false friendship leaves a bitter aftertaste. If he encounters resistance, the false friend quickly transforms himself into a fierce enemy, who insults and mocks his former *"friend."*

Some, especially when the friendship concerns boys and girls, behave like the peacock that attracts the female by fanning his tail. The ploy of these young people is just about as pitiful. Their overflowing sensuality makes one think of another Don Juan. However, this is not the conquering Don Juan of old, since today, with the great relaxation of morality in our society, there are hardly any obstacles to the conquest, but rather it's the pathetic Don Juan, the collector of hearts. This perpetually unsatisfied person imagines himself as "recreating his existence" at every moment, with each new conquest, thereby cultivating the illusion of living an eternal youth, thanks to the constantly renewed discovery of another immature *"love."*

CHAPTER 21

What if you've allowed yourself to be trapped?

In *The Song of Songs*, the young woman in love regularly proposes that she meet with her beloved. It's not without risk on her part, since her brothers are very jealous, and have been given the task of ferociously guarding her virginity. When they come upon one of these encounters by chance, they cry, *"Seize those little foxes who are playing in our vineyard."* The vineyard is their sister, and the little foxes are the boys who are not insensitive to her charms.

In our lives too, the little foxes can become invasive. One must fight a fire in the very beginning. It is almost impossible, too, to stop a rushing torrent that is hurtling down a mountainside. So if you are faced with an unclear proposal, and you say to yourself, *"I'm going to explore this area; after all. We have to have many experiences in life, but I'll stop whenever I want,"* you are playing with fire, or you are foolishly hoping to be able to stem the tide of swiftly rising waters.

The tale is told that in certain countries there once were goats that breathed through their ears. I don't believe this to be true; however, I know that our hearts breathe through our ears, by receiving the thoughts of others that flow through them. It's best not to breathe the air of dubious words or suggestions, since they could ultimately asphyxiate our entire heart.

Never put God between the parentheses, and don't ever agree to do something that is not in conformity with your morals. If you've already allowed yourself to be trapped, make a resolution never to remain in a similar situation again.

Sometimes the best decision is to make a complete break. You can't recover from taking drugs by continuing to hang around with those who smoke joints or pop pills or more. Sometimes, you need to have the courage even to make changes to where you live or work. St. Jerome, one of the first Christian authors, tells the story of a boy who decided to break up with a girl who liked to go to the orgies that were so popular toward the end of the Roman Empire. This had all its evil consequences, and the boy decided to leave for an expedition far away, that allowed him to forget his initial passion for that girl. Later, upon his return, he ran into the girl again, who said to him, *"Don't you recognize me? It's really me!"* He replied *"Really? But I am not the same person anymore."* The trip had brought about a profound change in him. St. Augustine, one of the first Fathers of the Church, explains in his Confessions that, in order to get over the grief of the loss of one of his best friends, he had had to move and go to Carthage.

Don't think that breaking with damaging friendships will be easy. People who have been kept in handcuffs still carry their marks on their wrists for some time afterwards. The memory of the pleasure that you may have felt will remain. It will take some time for the interior solitude that you must impose upon yourself to be able to completely satisfy you, and bring you other sources of pleasure. At that time, turn to true friends if it's possible, and also return to the road of personal prayer in order to heal.

The objection often made is to ask yourself if it's not ingratitude to break up a friendship, even if you've decided that its influence is negative, or to flee those people whose influence was not good, but with whom you've shared part of your journey, and often agreeably.

Don't forget to put your relationship to your God into the equation. With God, you might also have to take the idea of ingratitude into consideration, especially if your behavior was not what He expected of you. God is counting on you, because God loves you and wants your happiness.

CHAPTER 22

Concluding our reflections of friendship

I'm sure you realize that it's the quality of the communication between friends that makes friendship strong, and allows us to maintain it well. Gradually the sharing becomes more natural, and shows its effect on many different aspects of our lives, as though by osmosis. The opening of our hearts to one another in friendship allows an intense, mutual exchange of impressions, preferences, ideas, affirmations, and choices both positive and negative to take place.

Bees make their honey from a wide variety of flowers. In the same manner, we receive both good and bad from our friends, and that is where we must be able to distinguish the one from the other. This is how gold diggers act, as they spend the entire day sifting. They are separating the sand and gravel that they throw back into the river, while they carefully set aside the valuable gold dust and nuggets. Friendship will bring you some gold, but it will not always be completely pure or debris free!

The great witnesses to the Faith, those whom we call saints, often had very radiant personalities that greatly impressed those who knew them. As a result, others wanted to imitate them. However, some people even imitated their faults, their stuttering, for example or their unusual way of walking. The canal of friendship can sometimes become polluted by peculiar habits or by the acceptance of rash judgments or prejudices that we may pick up from our friends. It's certainly not a good idea to add the faults of our friends to those that we already bear ourselves. It's actually the reverse that should take place as each friend inspires the other to reach for greater heights of virtue. So it's necessary to accept and bear with the faults of our friends, but it would be ridiculous for us to adopt those faults as our own or worse yet, to pass them on to others around us!

Here, I'm only speaking of those faults that are rather insignificant. You'll surely understand that, as far as actual vices are concerned, we must neither excuse them in our friends, nor adopt them ourselves. We would surely go quickly to the aid of a friend who was the victim of a fall while we were mountain climbing or biking together. If we saw a neighbor fall victim to a heart attack, we would just as quickly call 911. Just so, a true friend would not shrink from confronting a serious fault, or vice, or sin in his friend. The beautiful medieval tale of the salamander tells us that this animal not only did not fear fire, but thought that it could actually put it out by lying on top of it!

Vice ruins friendship and that is undeniable. If it's only a question of a passing fault, another chance can be given. But if it's something serious and lasting, it will be the death of the friendship. We have to, and must realize, that a friend who wants to lead us into evil <u>is no longer a friend</u>, but has become an enemy, and we must no longer pursue that friendship. If the one we love is vicious, so will be our friendship. We would need to seriously question what kind of fascination such a troubled personality might hold for us.

Sometime it happens that a friendship is founded more on a commonality of interests than on any particular sentiment. Our society is often structured so as to facilitate what we call a *"business friendship."* Let's not forget that if the Bible has beautiful words regarding friendship, it also tells us to be wary of the kind of relationship that is strictly for personal gain or profit. Nothing prevents us, however from gradually transforming a working relationship into a true friendship at some point.

I can say from personal experience that friendship makes us grow. This is surely one of the reasons that the Bible calls it one of the many kinds of *"blessings"* that God gives to people for their happiness. *"The one who loves God will also be capable of maintaining a good friendship."*

CHAPTER 23

Should we impose sacrifices on ourselves?

There's a wonderful legend that says that, if one is able to open an almond, write a message on the seed, close it again without damaging it, and plant it that way, all the almonds which that future almond tree produces will have the same message written on them. Just so, before adopting a certain exterior attitude or position, we must start by changing ourselves within. Our exterior must be born from our interior. This is especially true for everything having to do with education. We can certainly impose discipline and demand things by force, but if these demands and values aren't interiorized, all of our efforts will be for nothing. The heart, our heart, is truly the source of all our actions.

Your fidelity to God in your friendship with Him will produce fruits that will be easily identifiable like the almonds from the tree of which we just spoke, if it is deeply established and firmly anchored within you. St. Paul went so far as to say to his friends, *"It is no longer I who live, but Christ who lives within me."*

Now I'd like to give you some advice on the question of sacrifice. If you can fast, it would be a good idea for you to do that sometimes, and particularly during the times of year when our Church recommends sharing and moderation regarding our food and drink. It's good to be able to control your appetite.

Some people, however, impose exaggerated sacrifices upon themselves, which is not something desirable. It's not a good idea to fast too much when you are very young, since it needlessly weakens you. Did you know that deer have a hard time running well on two different occasions? One is when they have eaten too much, and are too fat, and the other is when food is scarce and they are too thin. When we have eaten too well, self-control is difficult; this is also true when we are too tired and weak. An excess of fasting or work can weaken both our bodies and our wills.

All things considered, it would be better to dedicate yourself to tiring work, than to impose a fast upon yourself. It's better to go and put yourself at the service of the sick and those who need you than to deprive yourself of a meal. The former is by far superior to the latter. It would also be better to maintain more strength than necessary than it would be to fall into a weakened state that would be harmful to you.

Christ advised his friends, *"Eat what is served to you"* (Lk 10:8). That is very good advice. Be satisfied with what you are given, whether you like it or not. That's worth much more than forcing yourself to eat disgusting things as a means of penance and sacrifice. It's really good to be able to accept all kinds of foods, and to know how to affirm people and appreciate different dishes or foods prepared by others from various backgrounds. It's best not to show any displeasure when the food prepared by those who invite you into their homes is not to your liking, and is really difficult for you to eat. I really like the story in St. Bernard's life when he drank some oil instead of wine that a distracted monk had served to him. It was a better penance than if he himself had decided to do something for penance, since it wasn't according to just his own will.

When I advise you to eat what is served to you, I am excluding those foods that would be injurious to your health or cause an allergic reaction. It's also best to maintain a habit of sobriety and a good measure of control over your consumption of alcohol rather than depending on intense and extended periods of abstaining from it, and then some excessive binging. But if even moderate drinking drags you down and weakens your will to the point that you make bad decisions and engage in unhealthy behavior then you must use your best effort to maintain a constant abstention and a healthy sobriety.

As for sleep, you need to sleep at night according to your needs. That will allow you to be wide-awake during the day. If you are a morning person, this can be an extraordinarily productive time of day. The birds themselves give us a fine example of this!

The Bible tells us the strange story of Balaam's donkey (Num 22:22-35). His king had given this foreign prophet the task of going to the Israelite's camp and cursing them. This curse was supposed to have the effect of weakening Israel before the war that King Balak of Moab was going to wage against them. Faced with the insistence of his king, as well as his promises of rich rewards, the prophet finally decided to mount his donkey and set forth to accomplish his mission. However, God sent a messenger, who sword in hand, was supposed to bar Balaam's way. This messenger was even supposed to kill Balaam if he tried to force his way through. The donkey saw the danger, but not his master. As a result, the animal refused to go on and Balaam beat her more and more violently with his stick. Finally she started to speak, reproaching the prophet for his violence and cruelty. Right away, Balaam understood the meaning of the situation. He bowed before the grandeur of God and ultimately blessed the camp of Israel instead of cursing it.

Sometimes we are inclined to act a bit like Balaam did with his donkey. When things start to go badly for you, you may have the idea of imposing some sort of hardship or punishment upon yourself, but this would be like beating the donkey, who didn't do anything wrong...it would be better for you to change your conduct and behavior from within.

CHAPTER 24

What place should others take in my life?

To stupefy everyone by incessant chattering, never to leave a minute free from activity, work, or some other meeting, or on the contrary, to flee all occasions of being among people; these are two extremes that it is best to avoid. Withdrawing from others is often perceived as disdain. Always seeking attention from others and imposing oneself on them demonstrates that one has nothing better to do with his time.

The Gospel tells us to love our neighbor as ourselves. We can certainly not flee from our neighbor and love him! However, in order to be able to love ourselves, we need to be able to have times of solitude, to take time for ourselves. *"Think also of yourself,"* said St. Bernard, *"and thus you will be strong enough to love others."* So if it happens that there is no urgent reason for you to be with others, or to receive them at your home, arrange your schedule so that you will have some quiet time for yourself. If it should happen that you are disturbed when you had hoped to be able to spend some time alone, however, put a smile on your face and make yourself completely available to your visitor, out of charity for him or her.

We know that some people are capable of unfortunate conniving. Those who have been bitten by a rabid dog are contagious; because their saliva can transmit the terrible illness they have contracted to others. Certain conversations and encounters can be contagious. Some other encounters have no other goal than to allow us to relax a bit, and to be able to freely laugh and joke. That kind of harmless meeting with friends can be very beneficial for us.

Participating in meetings or larger assemblies is often something that is necessary for us to do. Visiting with others maintains and develops our relationships with them. These are good things, so don't hesitate to be active in this way, however, it is distressing to see that some people always leave the organization of activities to others, and never seem to get involved in the life of the group themselves.

There are some encounters that stand out among others. It's good to be in the company of those who have interesting experiences to share. The vine that is planted among olive trees gives, it is said, produces delicious grapes that have a slight taste of olives. Just so, we are shaped by our encounters. We profit by the virtues of others, form their intuitions, their research, their intelligence. That is why being in the company of many different people can enrich us by providing a great diversity of points of view.

In our conversation, simplicity, kindness and politeness will always be appreciated. Who has not been a little annoyed by those individuals who create a lot of drama around the least little thing they have to say? Some people are so theatrical that everything is calculated so they can gain maximum benefit for themselves; their manner of walking, the number of their steps, their vocal intonations and pitch, their glances...all this theatre can sometimes ruin a good meal, an evening out, or a moment with friends. I advise you to try to adopt for yourself a joyous serenity, a calm outward aspect, and a good dose of humor in your encounters with others. Those who have sad faces are not fun to be with! *"A saint sad is a sad saint."* Don't forget that the Bible tells us *"Rejoice Always"* (Phil 4:4) and that the Lord himself wanted the apostles to have within them all the joy that He had come to bring into their lives (Jn 15:11). That joy is not at all expressed by the cynical sniggering of the person who *"shoots at anything that moves,"* with his acid remarks. If your tongue has a habit of being too quick, it would be good to make the effort to bring it under control, and not to be one of those people who spends his time shooting down others one by one.

While continuing to maintain a rich interpersonal life, I advise you to also love solitude. It's quite amazing to see to what extent today's society seeks to escape solitude, in every way possible. Just look around at the vast number of people whose ear pods tell you they are plugged into some kind of music or media to ward off silence! Yet, it is solitude that enables you to construct your own identity. It allows you to acquire to a greater extent that emotional maturity that is not fully reached in your adolescence. An immature emotional life will hardly leave you with any choice but to mimic the kind of cliché you may hear in the latest sitcoms or reality TV. However disagreeable they may be, the experiences of boredom and solitude are actually formative—they allow you to become aware of the passage of time, and to take the time to ponder the great questions of life, such as *"Why am I living? Who am I? What vocation or state of life am I called to?"* Time spent in solitude will give you the opportunity to come face to face with yourself in your own personal search for truth.

If you find that this time taken in solitude is unbearable for you, don't hesitate to ask yourself these questions, *"Why is it so difficult for me to be alone? Am I at peace with myself? What is my true vocation in life?"*

Never to have the opportunity to spend time alone and in silence, to fill all the moments of your life with constant noise, continuous meetings or a succession of purely emotional encounters, leaves something incomplete in your personality.

At the moment when huge crowds needed Him, at a time when hundreds of sick people were gathered in hopes of receiving comfort from Him, the Lord disappeared for entire nights, spending them alone on the mountain. This trait stunned the disciples, who reproached Him for it (Mk 1:35-39). Later, however they received from the Master the express invitation to act in the very same way, *"Come,"* he said to them, *"spend some time alone, and rest a while."* (Mk 6:31).

CHAPTER 25

May we follow the latest fashion trends?

St. Paul himself, in his reflections on the conduct of Christians of his time advises us in his letter to Timothy, 2:9 to dress properly. Hygiene and cleanliness are seen as a sign of respect toward others. The Bible, in its ancient requirements for the priests of the temple, required an irreproachable cleanliness, which was the sign of perfect interior cleanliness and honesty.

Styles change, and clothes are adapted to the circumstances and occupations of the person; that's natural. If you are invited to an upscale evening event, you would obviously not choose to wear the same kind of clothing that you would if you were going to clean out your grandmother's basement. Pay attention to your dress, especially if you are seeking a job, or attending a more formal event, including the Mass!

There is nothing wrong with elegance and good taste when your goal is to be nice to others. It's a question of degree, as with so many other things in life. Here too, though, it's best to be on the side of simplicity and modesty.

Spending a lot of time creating unusual hair-do or dying your hair so it looks *"just right,"* in the long run is kind of silly and unproductive. I'd like to see the young people who are following my advice be the best-dressed in their group of friends, but at the same time, dressed as simply as possible and not be a slave to brand names. In other words, don't overdo it, but do what is necessary to be presentable!

CHAPTER 26

How should you speak to God?

When I was a child, I could never go to the doctor without him asking me to stick out my tongue for him to look at. I was fascinated by the idea that he could know if I were in good health or not, just by looking at my tongue!

Our words give many signs as to the health of our interior lives. If you have a bad fall and something hurts a lot, you instinctively put your hand on that area. The tongue acts similarly regarding love. If you are close to God, you will often speak to Him in brief, loving terms. You'll be like the bees, and everything you do will remind you of the honey of His presence.

God is infinitely close to you; often it's you who distance yourself from God! In order to talk with God, you don't have to use fancy words or get into different postures or positions when you pray. You can meet God so intimately, like a lover who whispers in the ear of his beloved. God is like the morning dew. God is a sweet Presence permeating your entire existence.

So I invite you to imagine your relationship with God as sweet and tranquil. Don't always use the same format in speaking to Him. Be simple. It's not in the magic of the spoken word that prayer resides, but rather in the quality of the relationship that you have with God your Father!

CHAPTER 27

How can you show respect for others?

How easy it is for unkind words regarding others to escape our mouths! Often it happens, without our having a bad intention, nor do we consider the consequences of what we are saying. However, with unkind words, it's hard for us to know what their effects might be; sometimes they spread like a big grease stain does on our clothes! Some words are really venomous, and although they may appear to be funny at first, or welcome when they are spoken about others, we find them much more difficult to accept when we are the brunt of them, and we then realize how much evil can come from them. The consumption of certain foods causes a bad odor to remain on one's breath. Sometimes these hateful words are spoken under our breath, discreetly, confidentially. They are infinitely more venomous that way! The sharper the point of a spear, the more deeply it penetrates into the skin! Those who think they've been inspired to say something humorous while demolishing the reputation of someone else don't really know what humor is. Conversations should bear more resemblance to the work of bees that are gathering to make honey than to the buzzing of a swarm of wasps attacking some dead animal.

If you're a witness to that kind of verbal aggression, try to find a tactful, and if possible, humorous way to make your listener understand that you don't take part in that kind of entertainment. It's true that people have a right to joke with others...but to exercise one's talent by using stinging mockery about the weaknesses of others is hardly a way to apply the virtue of love of neighbor. Derision and cynicism are particularly cruel and contemptible. The desire to be disrespectful of another's personality and personal integrity is a fault that must be recognized in others and in ourselves.

That certainly doesn't mean that you have to forego being humorous! Joking, using a play on words, teasing, including in order to point out little faults of our friends, are excellent things because they can add much to the ambiance of an encounter, and also show charm and intelligence. Humor skillfully used is an intelligent way to love others. The important thing here is to use sufficient tact and good taste to avoid the kind of verbal SLIPS that I mentioned earlier. Let's not be afraid of having fun! St. Louis himself, who was known to be extremely virtuous, did not like his monks to speak of religious subjects after a meal. On the contrary, he suggested that they have some fun, tell jokes and relax, so that each one could express himself with amusing frankness, which creates an amicable atmosphere in a group. We will have all of eternity to pursue our encounter with God and our ever-deeper discovery of Him...let us not think that relaxing with our friends in this way is a waste of time!

CHAPTER 28

What about our rash judgments of others?

"Judge not, and you will not be judged," the Lord reminds us in the Gospel of St. Luke (LK 6:37). *"Condemn not and you will not be condemned."* The Gospel often returns to the idea that judging others is very displeasing to God. In a very strict sense, God alone can judge us correctly, that is, in any case, not condemnation but an act of love. Each of us, then, should mind our own business first. We always have a desire to pay attention to other people's onions, probably because our own irritate our eyes, and in the end make us cry! It's so much easier to list the faults of our neighbors than to admit our own imperfections! Why is that?

Perhaps you are sometimes tempted to judge others negatively because you are bitter. First, then, you must renounce that bitterness in order to acquire greater clarity of vision. It's possible that pride is guiding your way of seeing things. The more we tear down others in our thoughts and words, the more we elevate ourselves in our own estimation. It's the work of the classic put-down process! The Pharisees began their prayer by thanking God first of all for not having made them women, and then for not having made them thieves or sneaks like some of those surrounding them.

At other times, without being either bitter or proud, you can experience some satisfaction in considering the faults of others, in order to savor ridiculousness, and to gloat over their failings in areas in which they believe themselves to be gifted. It's always amusing to see the hunter caught in his own trap.

At certain times, you may reassure yourself by stating very publicly that you are far from being the only one to have a particular fault that you have detected in yourself. This logic has its limits; when five people commit a particular sort of crime that in no way absolves or diminishes their responsibility for committing an additional homicide. At still other times, you might be curious about the little failings of others. It can also happen that you may be led to judge with passion by thinking that what you love is remarkable, and what you detest is heinous. Your point of view therefore can influence you and be singularly lacking in objectivity, don't you think? And still at other times, jealousy, fear, or ambition can contribute to the birth of your suspicions and of the negative judgment you make of others. What remedy can you apply to this evil that is so common in life?

Those who are addicted to drugs are sometimes subject to grave hallucinations. For them, detoxification is more than urgent and it will be a long and difficult process.

The antidote to making errors in judgment is kindness on the behalf of others. Everything looks yellow, they say, to those who are infected with jaundice. The sin of rash judgment of others is a kind of spiritual jaundice. Kindness will always give the benefit of doubt to every situation, while at the same time avoiding too great a naïveté. If a given action can have five possible interpretations, it would be very kind of you to ultimately choose the best motive for it.

It's a good thing that St. Joseph did not judge his young spouse with scandalized severity when he saw that she was pregnant before their marriage! Even if others do upset you, force yourself calmly and dispassionately to examine all of the angles that come into play in the situation at hand. Christ on the cross remarked that those who put the nails into his hands and feet did not know what they were doing. (Lk. 23:34)

So, can we never judge our neighbor? No we can't; it is God who will do it. It's true that judges pronounce sentence on criminals, but it's also true that the justice of humans is often imperfect. It is not forbidden to have doubts about your neighbor, or to mistrust him or her for good reason. Sometimes it's even a matter of common sense to do so. However, we can never know the hearts or minds of others.

By paying attention to the way you think of others, you can avoid these kinds of negative judgments. This does not prevent you, of course, if you have certain responsibilities in that area, from supervising those in your care in a realistic manner, and to correct them when correction is needed and necessary, but to always do it with love and kindness.

CHAPTER 29

Is it a mortal sin to slander someone's character?

We have seen that the hasty and negative judgments that we sometimes make regarding others can produce pernicious effects. Another fault that is equally harmful is slander. Here we are speaking about malicious talk, which, although undoubtedly not always unfounded, never does any good to the one about whom we are speaking. We habitually underestimate this fault though it is a very serious one. I affirm that the person who destroys the good reputation of his neighbor commits a fault that he must recognize, and he is under the obligation to make up for the evil that he has done. Slander is nothing other than a kind of spiritual homicide.

I implore you not to take pleasure in slandering anyone, either directly or indirectly. Avoid, in this situation, attributing any imaginary faults or vices to your neighbor. There is nothing that obliges you to publicize the faults that you do find in him or her, nor to exaggerate what you may have noticed. Slander can sometimes masquerade as an amusing, spirited conversation. We pretend to really like the person we are speaking about, *"but...just the same, if the truth be told..."*

Let's see things as they really are. Because one of the guests at the party to which you were invited had too much to drink doesn't mean he is necessarily an alcoholic. One occasion doesn't constitute the rule. St. Peter wasn't a total brute because he used a sword in defending Jesus on the Mount of Olives. We must also mistrust judgments founded upon observing the habitual actions of someone. St. Mary Magdalene must certainly have been called by many derogatory names, rather than by her real name at one point in her life. However, that didn't prevent her from receiving from Christ, the honor of being the first witness to the Resurrection, after her conversion.

The Pharisee proclaimed his own personal goodness before God and judged the Publican to be a man who was irremediably lost, and confirmed in his faults. And yet, that tax collector came away from his prayer *"justified"* because he acknowledged his sin and asked the Lord for mercy. One single instant is enough for God to completely convert someone, so how can we dare to decide that he is *"irremediably lost?"* The days, which have passed, must not judge the days of the future. We can never consider that a person is irretrievably lost without being in great danger of lying. We can state, if we have to speak of it at all, that this person has had some difficult moments, that he or she has made some bad choices, even that they still act badly today, but we can never draw from that any peremptory and definitive conclusions regarding his or her future.

As I often say, however, neither should we be ridiculously naïve by calling good that which is evil! To suggest that someone who truly has the tongue of a viper is just expressing herself frankly and spontaneously is ridiculous. In order to avoid slander, we need not go so far as to approve of the faults and failings of others. Do not hesitate to truthfully denounce what is wrong. However, in allowing yourself to reproach someone for his faults, it is necessary to consider the interests of the person you're addressing. First of all, one should seek out the person in question, while avoiding spreading gossip about him to third parties. This could give them the wrong idea. In the conversation you seek, it is well to be completely truthful in your words, without any exaggeration.

I remember a particular situation that occurred once with a group of young people who were in my care. I was obliged to make certain remarks to a boy and girl who appeared to be in love on the subject of the propriety of the degree of affection that they were showing one another in public. I had to be sure not to exaggerate things. I was conscious of the fact that, as I was admonishing them, my tongue was like the scalpel of a surgeon. When making an incision, the surgeon must be very skillful in order not to cause irreversible damage to nerves or tendons. In these kinds of delicate circumstances, it is also a good idea to address the fault in question, rather than to risk overwhelming the person responsible for it by attacking his or her character. I have also observed many verbal *"slips"* in conversations concerning politics, or perhaps regarding foreigners who may not be too well liked. Judgments can be very harshly pronounced in these cases, and that too is a lack of good judgment. When you hear words that are going to do harm to someone, help the speaker to nuance or reframe his words, but try to do so tactfully, so that he too may accept your message.

CHAPTER 30

A few reflections on how we should talk

Our speech is very revealing of who we are. Is your speech characterized by frankness, kindness, and respect, or by pretense, sarcasm, cruelty or mockery? Strive always to be a friend of the truth, because your God is a God of Truth, as Psalm 30 reminds us. Don't hesitate to correct an unkind word that might escape you, either immediately if you're aware of it, or by returning later to correct a certain stance that you may have wrongly taken.

There are many dangerous ways to hide the truth. A frank simplicity is always preferable to a kind of sneaky innuendo. A lie is often a means of escape, and is a form of cowardice.

In writing his <u>Confessions</u>, St. Augustine describes what he felt at the death of his friend in heart rendering sentences. In his grief, he stated that life horrified him; he could not bear to live, and from then on he was only half of what he had formerly been; he would have preferred to die, and have his friend remain in the world.

In a later work, Augustine returned to this subject, regretting his treatment of it. He maintained that he had exaggerated his feelings, and that he had used an emotional style that was painfully exaggerated. It was truly sensitive on his part to admit that, since no one would have challenged, him for having his grief in such a passionate manner.

To be careful of the way we express ourselves doesn't mean that we have to agree with everyone. It is important to express your own opinion, and to disagree with the opinion of others when necessary. However, that can be done without the vehemence, which can make an exchange of opinions impossible. The Greek philosophers advised us to *speak little.* I interpret this advice not by thinking that we need to restrain the number of our words, but rather that we should avoid speaking useless words that can be hurtful to others.

As a last piece of advice, I suggest that you avoid asides with others, whisperings and meaningful looks. These behaviors are not exactly unkind, but they lead sensitive people to believe that others are mocking them, which is not very kind.

CHAPTER 31

A few words about leisure time

Don't be afraid to take time to relax regularly. The story is told of a holy man of excellent reputation who startled a hunter who had come to meet him. The hunter found the man stroking the head of a little partridge that he was taking time to tame. This hunter expressed his indignation at the top of his lungs, saying that such an activity was not at all worthy of the reputation of the holy man, and that he had expected to find him giving himself to prayer, study or deep discussion. He professed himself to be quite shocked by such infantile behavior. The holy man listened, and then asked the hunter why he didn't always keep the string of his bow taut.

"Because if the bow is always kept taut, it loses its strength and elasticity. Then, when the time comes to use it, it is less powerful."

"It's the same way with me," said the man of God. "I too need to relax. It makes my prayer and study more effective in the long run. "

The holy man was absolutely correct; it's a real vice never to want to take time for yourself and to condemn those who do so!

So don't be afraid to get out into the fresh air, play basketball, go hiking, spend a fun evening with friends, play a musical instrument, work out, or participate in some other type of activity. You have your youth to take time to develop your body; tomorrow it will be too late. You'll find that there are activities available for all tastes and temperaments, and taking part in them will also make you more dynamic in your Christian life!

From tennis to martial arts, and from chess to rock-climbing—obviously, you have to be careful not to overdo it, because if you exhaust yourself, you'll achieve the reverse effect of what you're looking for during your relaxation time. After playing five or six hours of chess, for instance, one is completely wiped out. Interminable sets of tennis can also leave you dragging. After all, there is life after leisure.

So don't let your free time activities enslave you and take over your life. Get the most out of them, savor the intensity of the present moment when you take part in them, but learn to know when to stop as well!

CHAPTER 32

Forbidden Games

Certain pastimes are worth a little more reflection on our part. Spending a large amount of one's money on gambling, or regularly frequenting casinos is not just an example of an agreeable pass-time, but rather something that can become a dangerous habit. As a result, many of these games are even regulated by law.

What is wrong with such activities? One can make a lot of money, not by an intelligently developed strategy, but as a result of pure luck. In this light, we realize that it's not really very moral to win sums of money that we have not earned. Above all, these pastimes are not actually a means of relaxation, nor are they a nice way to spend your free time. Serious players take part in them with a real degree of passion, and even anguish. Take a good look at these players; they are totally absorbed in their passion. It is forbidden to laugh, speak, or even cough when they are in the midst of a game. What a shame to invest so much energy in such an unworthy activity!

CHAPTER 33

Saturday night fever

The parties to which you may be invited can be very different from one another. It is a good idea to take a sober look at what is happening there. By definition, these parties or *"happenings"* take place at night, and drag on to the wee hours. It is very possible that certain things will take place at them that could not have been predicted beforehand. Spending the night dancing does not allow you to be very fresh the next day, that's obvious. It's kind of too bad if someone is depending on you that day; you should be aware of that when you factor an evening out into your schedule. It's a shame to turn your nights into days and then not be very productive during the day itself.

Mushrooms, by virtue of their spongy nature, attract pollution and radioactivity. As an example, harvesting them would not at all be advisable in the area of Chernobyl or Japan where there have been nuclear disasters. All night parties can have a similar effect sometimes, presenting difficulties that go beyond their original purpose. For example, drugs, alcohol and relaxed, loosened up and irresponsible attitudes can find fertile ground there. So be careful because in some cases, passing feelings of euphoria combined with loud pounding music, a general party atmosphere and the resulting fatigue can result in undesirable, unwanted or exploitive behavior on your part or that of others.

Take a good look at how you've used the time that God has given you, comparing it to the lives of some of the good men and women of our times. It offers us a good point of reference, which is not meant to disturb or upset you, but to allow us to come to a clearer realization of things. Think about it!

Are you making a judicious, sensible and well thought-out choice? While you were dancing and having a good time, some people were living through very dramatic events, a fire or earthquake, and some were preparing to meet their Creator face to face. Monks arose very early in the morning to sing the Glory of the Lord in the first prayers of the day. During the party or "*bash*" children were hungry, while others were exploited. You spent some of your time, your energy, and your youth during that night. Well, why not, if it was a lovely evening? But was it really a lovely evening for you? Did you really make good use of your time?

Does this moment of reflection perhaps inspire you to use some of your time, your talents, your youth, and your energy for good causes and the service of others? Or do you wish to ignore these thoughts in favor of re-living ups and downs at the party? You may then have something to really think about!

CHAPTER 34

So, do you have to forget all about having fun?

I don't want you to think that I would prefer to see you praying the Rosary all night long for those who are suffering, rather than meeting up with your friends for an evening of fun. This would not be at all consistent with what I told you in the beginning of this book. I want to reassure you on this point; the primary function of your free time activities is to relax you, and that is a real necessity. Going to parties can be a pleasant experience for you and can also bring satisfaction and joy to the friends who have invited you. That's another good reason to take part in them.

The witnesses to the faith whom we call saints, although many had a great sense of humor, and some were even inclined to play harmless pranks, were not always interested in spending their nights in a dance hall. However, they did go to parties, relaxed, and had fun, many times just because it brought so much pleasure and happiness to their friends. In those cases, the different people that they might have met had little ill effect on them. They were like those great granite rocks by the ocean, battered by storm waves, but always remaining solid and strong.

Happily, the interior life is not immediately dissolved by the questionable circumstances that may surround us. Often, it's actually the opposite; a big fire grows larger when it's fanned by wind, but the little ones go out if we merely blow on them. The ideal is that your interior life is sufficiently strong and blazing within you so that you need not fear its being snuffed out by little temptations, but on the contrary, that your interior life may grow steadily, even when you encounter people who are not leading very exemplary lives.

CHAPTER 35

Pay attention to the details

In the Song of Songs, the young man gives a wonderful description of the young woman whom he loves. He expresses his admiration for the beautiful eyes of the *"beloved,"* but also for her beautiful hair. It's true that the eye is *"the mirror of the soul,"* and the symbolic importance of the eyes has often been studied. But the hair, even though it contributes to a person's beauty, has usually been much less symbolic and evocative.

In this Biblical book, the young man represents God, in love with humanity and the girl is our human condition. I like to interpret this text by imagining that God is not only dazzled by the beauty of the eyes, or in other words, of the magnificent works performed by very virtuous and selfless persons, but also by the hair; in other words, by much more ordinary people, like you and I. If God is in love with humanity, it is not just the great saints who attract Him, but it is also the imperfect and needy ones among us. This love of God for each person exalts us and gives a wonderful meaning to the least of our actions.

We can dream about giving God everything; our time and all our talents, and we can imagine that we would be prepared to suffer the most awful torments for His sake. We would give God our eyes, if necessary. But while you wait for the events to present themselves that would require great things of you, or even your faithful witness to martyrdom, be happy to offer *"your hair."* In other words, be valiant in everyday life and the little difficulties that tire you day after day.

God is in love with this dimension of your person too. These little patient acts of daily fidelity; the headache suffered with a smile so as not to break the ambiance of an evening with friends, the toothache, the bad mood of someone or other that you bear with in a good natured fashion, a treasured glass or family heirloom that is broken, someone who casts a scornful glance at you, the little sacrifice you make in not going to bed late in order to be available in the morning, the disapproval of others when you take part in a religious activity...all of these *"little sufferings"* can in the end amount to a treasure of spiritual riches that will allow you to make progress spiritually.

I like the idea that the great mystics also cooked and did the dishes. The great occasions to serve God present themselves rarely, but the little ones are quite frequent. If you can live the Gospel by being attentive to the little details of your life, you will be able to follow the Lord who came to share our paths in the simplicity of our human condition much more closely.

CHAPTER 36

How can you judge things properly?

The majority of philosophers tell us that it is our reason that makes us human. Why then is it so rare to find truly reasonable persons on our journey here on earth? At least, that's the impression we often have.

Others seem so unreasonable to us, which is, of course, not the case with ourselves. Far from it! We like people to appreciate our jokes, but we are very sensitive when someone dares to make a joke about us. We find that others are not very accommodating, but we imagine ourselves to be so to a really exemplary degree. If someone who we consider subordinate displeases us, we don't miss any opportunity to humiliate that person or to offer correction. On the other hand, if we like someone, we often easily excuse that person's faults. There are some very virtuous children whose parents don't seem to be able to tolerate them at all just because they may be cross-eyed, or because they don't have a very pleasing physique. There are other really physically beautiful children who, although they are actually vicious-minded and mean, have all manner of excuses made for their behavior.

We instinctively prefer the rich to the poor, even though their moral character may not be as well founded at all. We prefer to receive well-dressed people into our homes. We demand that our rights be respected, but are disturbed when others lay claim to their rights. We expect to be treated in accord with the dignity due our position in society, but we would like to see more simplicity in those well-known people whom we know. We have plenty of reasons for complaining about others, but we can't understand how anyone could criticize us!

We resemble those mythical birds that were reputed to have two hearts; we have a heart that is tender, loving, and attentive for ourselves, and a strict rigid and vindictive heart when it comes to others. We use, as they say, two completely different systems of measurement.

I want to give you some difficult advice: be just. Know how to put yourself in the place of others; imagine you are the seller while buying, and the buyer while selling. Do you act toward others the way you want them to act toward you? That is the law of the Gospel, and the Golden Rule.

The Emperor Trajan was reproached for his familiarity with people while he was the emperor of Rome. *"I understand,"* he answered, *"but I have to act toward my subjects, as Emperor, the way I would like the emperor to act if I myself were a subject."*

CHAPTER 37

Desire and Reality

We are beings with certain desires. We have already seen that our desires can sometimes lead us in dangerous directions, which will certainly not help us to grow. I'm speaking not only of dubious desires here, but also, for example, of a desire to have intense spiritual experiences, to have a strong feeling of the presence of God, or of experiencing ecstasies in prayer.

Generally speaking, don't fix your desires upon objectives that are so unattainable that they will ultimately make you feel, unfulfilled in your life. If a young man has the desire to attain a particularly sought-after job, he must also be prepared to modify his goal if it doesn't work out, and put that dream to rest.

I can imagine an adolescent wanting, for instance, to become a fighter pilot. It's an ambitious goal, and there are a certain small number of people who will attain it. However, he could ultimately be eliminated from the running by the results of a vision test, while all along it had appeared that he would be able to realize his dream. In all practicality, a young man who is not gifted in mathematics in high school has little chance of realizing that particular goal in any case. If he were living for that dream, he would quickly become bitter.

If a young, newly married woman dreams seriously about becoming a Carmelite nun, she risks being forever miserable in her marriage. If, nailed to my bed by the flu, I insist that I must be able to preach in my cathedral, or participate in a televised debate; this desire is pointless, because I am not capable of realizing it. In this case, it would be well for me to concentrate on developing my patience, and not on making life miserable for those who are trying to care for me. We are sometimes like those pregnant women who have sudden overpowering cravings for cherries in autumn, or grapes in summer, or ice cream when the freezer is empty!

It's especially regrettable when we see someone in a position of responsibility who wants at all costs to be something other than what she is. It would be ridiculous for me, as a bishop, to start dreaming of being a Trappist monk living in magnificent solitude up in the Alps. It would be better for me to use my energy and imagination in fulfilling my role as a bishop to the best of my ability. I will not ever become more intelligent than I actually am. It's much better for me to use my intelligence and attempt to develop my God-given talents to the maximum of my potential rather than dream of acquiring gifts that I will never have. Here I'm talking about desires that become a real preoccupation, not of those harmless daydreams that sometimes provide us with an amusing momentary escape from our routines.

Do not desire trials from God, either; rather, bear with those which life has in store for you, as they come along. Sometimes it happens that we dream of undertaking great trials for God which will never actually happen, while we aren't even capable of putting up with the difficulties of our daily lives. In our imaginations, we'd like to face great danger on a humanitarian mission to Africa, and, yet we allow ourselves to be conquered by the simple problems of our daily lives by not addressing them seriously and realistically.

Eating too much overloads the stomach and results in upsetting it. It's a good sign to have a good appetite, especially when one is young, but one must also be able to digest all that one has eaten! It's the same for the spiritual goals we set for ourselves. To suddenly decide to get up a half hour earlier each morning to meditate, to go to mass every evening, to spend two nights a week at prayer group meetings, to decide to fund the education of a child or seminarian, to read the gospel at lunchtime, or to spend your weekends on retreat; all of this, although you've never done anything of a religious nature beforehand, is too much to attempt all at once. I'm not saying it's a bad thing to have spiritual goals, on the contrary. However it would be better to take things more slowly and to make more achievable goals for yourself: in other words, *everything in due season."*

CHAPTER 38

A few words on marriage

Marriage is a great sacrament, affirms the Church in St. Paul's Letter to the Ephesians (5:32). In it, our Church sees one of the supreme ways of living out one's *"personal vocation."* In a certain way, marriage is actually the living source of the Church, because it permits the people of God to grow, generation after generation. It's a great shame that the Son of God is not invited to every wedding celebration on earth, as He was invited to the one in Cana. How abundantly the wine of gladness would then flow!

It's very common today to advise those who intend to be married to live deeply their mutual love. *"Husbands, love your wives as Jesus Christ loves His Church; wives, love your husbands as the Church loves its Savior,"* St. Paul tells us. The first effect of this love is an indissoluble union of hearts. *"Amour...toujours"*...(love forever.) Should we really believe this ancient rhyme? In cabinetmaking, if you press two pieces of fir together, provided that the glue is of good quality, it turns out than any break in the wood will be most likely to occur somewhere other than at the spot where the two pieces have been joined.

The marital union takes place, not only physically, but it is also a union of the feelings, emotions, and the hearts of the spouses. However, it's really not just a question of feelings, or even of the will. Marriage is a firm link that calls us to grow, while respecting the similarities and differences of each of the partners.

The second effect of this love is the proposal of the partners to live in fidelity to one another. It was the custom at one time for families to wear *"signet rings,"* on which the coats of arms of the houses of nobility were carved. These unique rings were used to seal and mark official documents. When he blesses the wedding rings of a betrothed couple, the priest ennobles their future home, and above all, seals their love in a concrete and visible way.

The third fruit of marriage is the promise to bring children into the world and to raise them in the Faith. That is in itself a magnificent goal. To partake in the creative action of your God is something really great.

CHAPTER 39

The appetites

Paying attention to what one eats is an excellent idea. Today we are more aware than ever before of the importance of the quality of the food we eat, and as well as of the necessity of maintaining a well balanced diet. However, even then, it is possible to have *"too much of a good thing."* In the euphoria of springtime, even the bees sometimes ingest excessive quantities of honey, rendering them sick enough even to die of an overdose of it. In the sacrament of marriage, its goods are enjoyed, not only in their unitive benefits, but, according to the design of the Creator, with the happy result of bringing into the world and the Church the great gift of children.

Now, the sin of gluttony is quite a disagreeable vice, and I know some people who, even before going to the table to eat, are already smacking their lips over what awaits them. In other words, *'Their God is their stomach,"* as St. Paul tells us in his Letter to the Philippines, (Ph 3:19). Would that, once having risen from the table, our minds do not remain fixed on what we have enjoyed there. All that I have said to this point can easily be transposed to apply to the domain of marital relations.

The human being is not the only animal who is faithful to his spouse. Nature is a wonderful book that displays many examples of fidelity to our eyes. I was amazed to learn the story of the elephant, for example, which, though a great and powerful beast, observes a remarkable fidelity and gentleness to his companion. In marriage, although it takes time for love to come to full flower, it is a limitless gift for the spouses to give one another, permitting each to grow and mature along with the other.

CHAPTER 40

Just a word on widows

(Widowhood in the days of Saint Francis de Sales was a prevalent reality in society. It was very common to all age groups, young adults included. In his original work this section was quite long. The advice given on this subject is difficult to transpose for our time; thus, this chapter has been considerably reduced.)

Each individual circumstance of our lives, even the most tragic, can ultimately bring a singular richness and an irreplaceable experience into the lives of the community of believers. I have often remarked that a heavy trial in life can create a spiritual experience that ultimately gives one an extraordinary capacity to understand and comfort the suffering of others. Those who have been widowed, then, can provide a magnificent service to their brothers and sisters as a result of having undergone that trial.

CHAPTER 41

A word for those who are considering marriage or the consecrated life

You know, it is not particularly wise to have multiple experiences before marrying. Investing itself in a succession of amorous relationships; each time thinking, *"This will be the one"*, ultimately exhausts the heart.

Maybe you've wondered about another possibility that lies in the happiness that comes from a celibate life given to God. This is a vocation that will fulfill you completely if you are called to it. One of the most beautiful manifestations of true love is found in turning all of your emotions and all of your availability toward your Creator, in order to live intensely in the service of your brothers and sisters, and to discover the road to happiness in so doing.

There are a variety of resources that are available to help you in that search, if you feel it is where God is calling you. It will also be extremely beneficial for you to choose a spiritual director who will help you to explore this call that is within you, and to see clearly that path that you should follow.

PART FOUR

How can you fight the
evil within you?

CHAPTER 1

The seduction of the world

It's very possible that your desire to deepen your Christian life and to make choices formed by that desire will draw negative comments and criticism from those around you. You may even be suspected of hypocrisy. Or, it may be said of you that you are taking refuge in the practice of virtue in order to compensate for your frustrations and your incapacity to form satisfying relationships with others. People will try to convince you that your choices are ridiculous, and they'll accuse you of trying everyone's patience. They will ask you if it doesn't bother you that you are spending the majority of your time with the *"little old ladies"* of the parish. They will ask you what right you have to consider yourself better than others, or superior to them.

This may surprise you, and even make you a little panicky the first few times you hear these things, thinking that you are going to lose your friends and find yourself alone with Christians who are not all that much fun to be with. Don't worry about that at all. It's not always easy not to behave in the same way as the rest of the world, it's true, but convince yourself of this truth; the people who criticize you in this way aren't doing so because of any special concern of theirs for you. Your true friends however infrequently you may be able to speak seriously with them, will respect your choices.

Isn't it strange to think how some people spend entire nights *"entertaining"* themselves by abusing a variety of drugs, and no one says a word, contending that we each have the right to make our own decisions, but your interest in religion or expression of faith may very well draw sharp criticism. Or, in another instance a weekend of reflection and retreat in a monastery will provide a great topic for jokes made at your expense.

The Lord loved this world, but loving the world does not mean accepting all that it does. Jesus Christ was criticized because His choices upset others. Some of the people of his time ridiculed Him or disregarded Him...writing Him off either as a strange ascetic or as a parasite. Some people will be shocked to find someone *"hung up on religion"* attending certain parties. However, the same people will judge his absence as sad and *"serious."* What difference does it make! We cannot please everyone! But this should not in any way cause us to despair. In addition, we ourselves must overcome the vulnerability that tempts us to judge the critics of religion harshly.

There are times when you will have the very painful feeling that you have been stabbed in the back. It's as though certain people are just waiting for you to make a mistake in order to rejoice over it. Just the same, don't give in to paranoia. After all, you are not the center of the universe! Even if you are less resistant to criticism regarding your religion than you are to your ethnic heritage or your dining preferences, it's not all that serious.

I repeat; let these worries go. I've already referred to the comets and the stars that shine with equal brilliance, reminding you those comets disappear very quickly. If you are accused of being an opportunist, remind yourself that hypocrisy and true virtue have many traits in common, but that, given time, they will be able to be distinguished from one another. If you know how to be truthful and sincere, eventually you will be appreciated anyway. Critics are like bats; during the day they are frightening, but they actually do very little damage. Be strong in your convictions, and persevere. You can remind yourself that in the end it is better to be the brunt of some criticism because of your choices; it will prevent you from having too exalted an opinion of yourself!

CHAPTER 2

You need to be strong

When we suddenly emerge from a dark tunnel, the light blinds us momentarily. However, we need that light.

When we find ourselves in a foreign country, even if the people are polite and friendly, we still feel a little out of place in the beginning. It's the same way when we make the choice to follow Christ more closely. We have to give up some of the trivial things that we're used to, and that can bring up feelings of discouragement and sadness within us.

If that happens, please don't be discouraged, and don't give up! You will surely find much more in your new choice than what you have left behind.

At first you may find it somewhat upsetting to have to give up some prestige, self-love, and vanity, but these are only lures that risk making you turn back. Look around you...the mountain of Christian perfection is extremely high.

"*Lord,*" you say, "*how can I do it?*"

Have courage.

Look closely at nature...when bees are just starting to form, they are called larvae...they don't yet know about flying into the mountains and fields and lighting or landing

250

on flowers to gather honey. But, little by little, they get stronger.

Maybe you feel a bit like a larva in your search for God? You look at the summit and challenge of Christian excellence of which the Beatitudes speak with a little perplexity. Once your desires and your initiatives start to take shape, though, that's when your wings begin to grow. One day we will be like the bees in the mountains when we will take flight. And in the meantime what do we do? Maybe it's best to be a bit like them; we can feed on the honey that the witnesses to Christ who've gone before us have left for us as a legacy.

CHAPTER 3

Have you undergone temptation?

What I would like you to do now is to imagine a typical story line found in an American sit-com or drama. One day, a good and beautiful young woman who is very much in love with her young husband receives a very disgusting message from a sexual deviant. This person makes an obscene proposition to her. His evil intentions are direct and quite clear. The development of the plot will now depend on our young woman. She can either accept this evil proposition, or she can categorically refuse to have anything to do with this sinister individual. In the future, if she happens to run into him by chance, her actions will once again be the result of the determination of her own will.

Why should I present such a banal scenario? It's because evil presents itself in just the same way to us. In the depths of our personalities, there is a sort of morbid fascination with evil that can express itself more or less clearly. The invitation either pleases us or not; it interests us or it doesn't. We can then decide either to consent to the invitation or not, and we can even find a certain pleasure in our consent.

If it's true that God has placed a number of talents in each of us, it's also true that we are each susceptible to a major sin, though not necessarily the same one. It is the principal fault against which our own particular personality struggles. We don't even know why this is, except that this is the way in which human nature is made.

It is certain that God knows each of us and understands this weakness of ours, which will last as long as we live. The challenge is not to allow it to enslave us. The battle and the suffering we endure as we face this major sin, which is within us, is at one and the same time a part of our greatness and our nobility as human beings. St. Paul himself, as well as many who came after him, confesses that he had suffered certain temptations for a very long time, which he does not describe in any greater detail than that. That we continue to desire to follow God in spite of our weakness; that is the great goal of our baptism. In this spiritual combat, different personalities have faced the enemy with different weapons. Although it's admittedly a rather extreme remedy, St. Francis of Assisi once threw himself into some thorn bushes, rolling in them in order to overcome his temptation!

Do not feel guilty just because you are feeling tempted; the temptation is not a fault in you. However, to declare yourself defeated before even doing battle -- that would be a great mistake. Referring back to my original scenario, a young woman cannot be blamed for being the target of a deviant. In real life, there can be another angle to my evil drama/sit-com. The young woman could call her husband, or the police, in order to put the stalker who is sending her these evil messages out of commission. This is not the case with us, however. Our temptations return because they are within us, and we can hardly even guess their source. However, they cannot harm us as long as they are displeasing to us, and as long as we do not give in to them.

Perhaps it will happen that you will give in one day. Here I'd like to point that there are two levels of your personality. There is always a kind of sleeping beast in each of us...and this is what has awakened. We often have the experience of an interior struggle between good and evil within us. St. Paul tells us, *"The evil I do not want to do, I do."*

Have you ever noticed that, on the day following a beautiful fire that you built in your fireplace, there are tiny cinders? If you return early in the morning, ten or twelve hours afterwards to look for the fire, you'll still find these tiny cinders burning, and you'll be able to easily light the fire again. This observation is also true of your *"interior fire."* Even after fleeing from all the flames of the temptations that might have overcome you, and even encumbered by the ashes of sleep, the cinder still burns. Those burning embers are your desire not to give in to the evil that is within you. It's what St. Paul calls *"building the interior person."*

CHAPTER 4

A commentary

There are some days when the will just seems to disintegrate, and the patient building of purity, gentleness, and clarity that we are trying to erect seem ready to collapse in one swift stroke. Temptation unfurls itself like a great storm, and it seems that nothing can resist it. A picture seen, and unexpected thought, a scene in a movie, a passage read, a twist in a conversation, can become overwhelming and unleash unexpected storms. Sometimes you don't even know if this spiritual battle is worth it, or if there's any sense in resisting. If this happens, don't think you're alone in fighting this battle. God does not flee from you when you experience serious temptation. Beneath the cinders of dark desires, the embers that will rekindle the fires of your life of virtue are still burning. In any case, these storms are like shooting stars...in the end, they will burn themselves out.

CHAPTER 5

Some ongoing thoughts for those times of "storm warnings"

Curiously, it's not always the times of the greatest temptations that create the most damage to our spiritual lives. Fortunately, we are stronger than we often believe ourselves to be. Know that, if you are facing a time of interior tempest, God will deprive you neither of his presence, nor of His help.

When there's a serious accident, the victim is sometimes unconscious, and the rescuers may think at first that he or she died. One of the first things that they will do in such a case is to discern whether the heart is still beating.

If it is, there's still a chance of reviving the person. Sometimes it happens that the violence of the temptations we face and experience seems to completely kill our willpower, and we are spiritually knocked out. We become spiritually unconscious. All that remains to discern is whether the heart is still beating, and that is most often the case. By that I mean that, in the deepest part of your being, your center or "*heart*" it is probable that you have not fully consented to what you are doing. As long as there is a

movement of refusal within you, a revolt, or a feeling of dissatisfaction, you are still spiritually alive. You can bounce
back to life quite quickly by engaging your willpower with
your entire being.

CHAPTER 6

What if the idea occurs to you to do something wrong?

The young woman who received the lewd invitation from the deviant of whom we recently spoke regarding temptation was not responsible for what happened to her. Now let's imagine that she meets a very attractive young man, and she abruptly decides to leave her first love. In that case, she would be responsible for that decision, don't you think?

It's also very possible for us to be the initiators of the temptations that assail us. If, for example, I know that, in the heat of competition during certain sporting events, I have the habit of getting carried away, and lose all self-control, it is certainly my responsibility to resolve this recurrent problem, or to forego the sport altogether. In the same way, if I know that when I meet a certain friend, I am very likely to be tempted to speak unkindly about another person, it's my responsibility to avoid getting involved in that type of conversation with him. If we're able to avoid altogether the occasion of what can lead to a certain fault, that's even better.

There are certain pleasures, not evil in and of themselves, which can pave the way for other ones that are much less innocent. Let's go back to the example of the young woman, and imagine that she's a big fan of country music. As a result, she often goes to a bar where young musicians play. In itself, there's nothing wrong here; however, if it's on just such an occasion that our young woman finds one of the guitarists quite attractive, and she wants to spend the weekend with him, it's not the music that is to blame, but the unfaithful desires that the attraction fostered on this occasion awakens in her. Knowing this, it would perhaps be better for her to simply listen to a country station on the radio, buy a CD, or down-load some of the music and avoid the bar in question.

If someone proposes to me the Machiavellian idea that I take revenge on someone who has harmed me, I can be quite tempted by it. If I don't take any action on it, I don't commit any sin; however, it's still not healthy to spend too much time thinking about it, because that could ultimately make me want to actually do it. It's best not to even entertain such temptations in one's imagination, even if we're sure that we won't follow up on them. The pleasure of imagining them is not yet a fault. However, as an example of what can happen, it might be good to remember that driving too fast on a slippery road often ends in skidding and sliding off of it.

CHAPTER 7

Survival kit for strong temptations

According to the Gospel, if you are the object of a strong temptation, the first thing to do is to act like little children do when they find themselves in danger; they run to the arms of their mothers or fathers. However, it is probable that this method, although perfectly founded upon the Gospel itself, is not enough. I suggest that you also work on yourself, in order to bring all your intentions and your will into conformity with those of Christ himself.

If Christ were visible alongside of you as He was for the apostles, it's likely that your behavior would be different. You would not want to disappoint this great Friend who wants to teach you how to be the best you can be. Do your utmost to have a positive outlook on things. If you think too much about the temptation that you want to reject, it will invade your entire imagination and your inner being. Fix your gaze unflinchingly on Christ, and on what He is calling you to be. I have often noticed that when a novice mountain climber becomes dizzy while attempting to scale a cliff, it's better to look up rather than to look down. Occupy your mind with other activities that will keep you in a positive frame of mind. If your thoughts are occupied, you will not continually fix them on the idea that you wish to reject from your mind

Seek the help of your spiritual director. It is already a proven therapeutic technique to speak openly about these problems, whereas remaining silent only increases their difficulty. God wants clarity and lucidity for you, which your director or any other person in whom you have full confidence can help to bring about when you confide in him.

All of this may still not be sufficient. In spite of all your efforts, the temptation may linger on, or return. In this case, tell yourself that you'll *wear it down eventually.* Don't become upset, and do not despair. Continue to ignore the troublesome idea as much as possible. Going back to our former scenario with the young woman about whom we spoke at length, we must imagine that she immediately throws the offensive letters from her tormentor into the garbage, that she hangs up the phone as soon as she hears his voice, and that she immediately deletes any internet message that has been sent. It's best that she not waste time thinking all day long about this harassment, lest she tremble each time the phone rings, a letter comes, or when she opens messages on her computer. On the contrary, it would be in her best interest to take advantage of the time she spends with her young husband, that she take pleasure in his loving presence, and that she does her utmost to make life happy with him. She should not try to discuss anything at all on the phone with the one who is harassing her, either. Rather, she should remain tranquil and at peace, and one day the man will lose interest, and those painful calls will finally cease. This scenario that I have presented is also possible for you to follow if it should ever be necessary.

CHAPTER 8

Resistance, resistance

The spiritual combat that you will need to fight against big temptations is, you see, already won if you fight it patiently with Christ at your side. But you will also face various little temptations. These are not really very dangerous, but it's their number which is more to be dreaded than their effect. Wild wolves are much more fearsome than flies, but being harassed in summer by a swarm of those pesky insects is extremely trying to one's patience.

One can easily enough dismiss the idea of murder—but those outbursts of anger that we feel mounting within us are more difficult to master. Many would hesitate to frequent areas of ill repute while on a trip to a big city, but turning on an "X" rated film, downloading some porn, or having a secret rendezvous with a local beauty while on vacation doesn't seem too serious to some. We would surely hesitate to poison the cup of someone we really dislike, but we have few scruples about attacking him with words. The majority of people I know would hesitate to commit a serious infraction of the law, but if they can get away without paying a highway toll, certain of my friends would have no qualms about doing that. Most of us wouldn't consider giving false witness in court, but lying a little with one's friends doesn't give us too much pause. It would be unwise to show up for work drunk, but one drink too many at a party seems to be something harmless enough. I don't wish the death of anyone, but I was pleasantly surprised to learn that a known tax evader was having problems. We surely don't want to be the bearers of false tidings, but we reserve to ourselves the right to be interiorly scornful of those we consider loathsome.

In short, it's all these little temptations that shape us too, day after day; causes of anger, suspicion, jealously, flirting, pride, etc. We readily admit that none of that is really very evil. However, we need also to arm ourselves for these smaller battles on secondary fronts. The advantage we have is that victory in these areas is often easier...but how?

CHAPTER 9

Don't make mountains out of molehills

When this whole variety of temptations to vanity, suspicion, unhappiness, jealously, envy, flirtation, and so on pass before your eyes and sometimes sting you on the cheek, or the nose, it's impossible for you to be totally insensitive to them. They're like flies on a stormy summer night. The best way to resist them is not to allow yourself to be tormented by them. You can be much stronger than all of these little temptations.

Just ignore these little attacks; let them buzz about your ears as much as they want; and if they should indeed sting you, it is not going to cost you your life! You can escape them in one swift movement. Don't attach too much importance to them, since, if you tried to decide which opposite virtues to adopt for each one of your little imperfections, you would wear yourself out in the attempt. In your mind, simply realign your will with that of the Lord. Make time to be with Him often, and there you will find great peace of mind. These little temptations must be treated like they are -- little!

CHAPTER 10

How to gain spiritual strength

Pay close attention to the passions that are within you. If they are negative, look for a way to *"turn them around."* Imagine, for instance, that you become aware of a sharp feeling of superiority within you that is directed toward others. You perceive their lack of intelligence, and this becomes an irritation for you. You find that it's a real trial for you to have to lower yourself to the level of their shallow conversation. In order to combat this attitude, it's important for you to concentrate on cultivating and developing a patient level of generosity toward others. Be attentive to the needs of those around you, and try to become enthusiastic about being with them and helping them. Try to become aware that to behave like a vain, spoiled brat is a ridiculous and immature way to act. Oblige yourself to battle your pride, and force yourself to act with simplicity by doing things that are in themselves humble. Offer to go and wash dishes or serve meals at a homeless shelter for instance. Then, when that feeling of self-superiority and scorn for others returns, you will already have begun to overcome it.

Maybe you find that you're inclined to lack generosity toward others. The idea of sharing what you have with those who may have less or are *"good-for-nothings"* seems repulsive to you. Remind yourself, then, that the gifts you have been given do not come from yourself, and that one day you will have to depend on others, too. You'll have to leave everything behind at the end of your life. Learn to admire those who do show proof of their detachment and generosity not only by their words, but more importantly, by their example and seek them out. Look for opportunities to participate in volunteering your time and resources that will engage you physically, spiritually, and financially.

If you are a young lady who is reading this, I want you to think about what I am going to say. You may find it amusing to use your feminine charms on young men whom you find attractive. Think about how much emotional damage these games can do to those upon whom you set your sights. Consider the value of the clarity and simplicity that exists in true friendship. Challenge yourself to set aside time to develop good relationships with a group of people, rather than fostering and repeating those flirtations that isolate you from others. It's better to know yourself well, and to take the offensive in the way you live your Christian life, rather than to be obliged to react when you're suddenly faced with temptations. This advice is not only for the young ladies, it is meant for you young men as well!

CHAPTER 11

About anxiety

Are you a worrier by nature? This can be a real problem, because anxiety often leads to many trials. The first of these may be a profound sadness. It's true that we can legitimately feel remorse for having done something wrong. Sadness can also spring from something independent of our own will, such as when we are poor, sick, or despised by others. It can also be caused by more personal reasons, such as feelings of depression, lack of the will to live, or discouragement that well up within us. Whatever the reason, when sadness begins to invade us, it rapidly submerges our entire interior life. It's a feeling that is difficult to deal with and one that we'd like to get rid of as soon as possible. It goes so much against our legitimate and sincere desire for happiness!

If you try to dispel your anxiety and sadness by following the counsels of the Gospel, you'll realize that things don't depend on you alone, but also on the support that God can give you. If you count only on your own resources, you'll believe that you can only find the strength to overcome your feelings of discouragement somewhere within yourself. In that case, if the sadness persists, and if the feeling of failure does not dissipate, the feeling of anxiety that's still there will become even more invasive. That will lead to a loss of self-confidence. This sets up a dangerous dynamic; a kind of *"vicious circle,"* since anxiety engenders sadness, which, in itself leads to an excess of anxiety!

In fact, there's nothing worse than the feeling of interior despair. Let me assure you that this is as serious an evil as any other. A country that has been ruined by an exhaustive civil war will be completely incapable of facing a threat from the outside. If you are in a state of *"interior war"* with yourself, you will never be able to confront the difficulties that life will surely bring you.

Anxiety often comes from the doubt we may feel of ever being able to free ourselves from evil and overcoming our difficulties. That goal sometimes seems, like a mirage, to always be just beyond our grasp. When a bird is caught in a net, the more it fights the net, the more entangled it becomes. The stronger our desire to be delivered from our anxiety, the more the latter grows. But our panic is as useless here as the efforts of the bird caught in the net. On the contrary, we must calm down and try to peacefully gather our wits. One of the most efficacious means of doing this is to invest our efforts in prayer. The writers of the Psalms have translated this battle against anxiety, and the appeasement of it that our encounter with God can bring, in extraordinary detail: *"Into Your Hands, Lord, I commend my spirit."*

Don't let worry and anxiety get the better of you. The more sad and anxious you are, the more subject you'll be to going from failure to failure and from dissatisfaction to despair.

Anguish does exist, and you have undoubtedly met it at times. Confront it, while at the same time seeking tranquility, and don't believe that dreaming about achieving peace of mind is just an illusion or an escape. It is such a great Gospel virtue that you'd be wrong to deprive yourself of it.

The peace which the Gospel speaks is not the absence of worries which a comfortable or stable situation produces, nor is it that peaceable characteristic that teachers appreciate so much in their docile pupils. It is rather a kind of serenity, a confidence in humanity and our Creator. It's an optimistic bet on the good that is within us—within you. It is also the conviction that God is loving and that God has put in the heart of each person just as in the dynamics of the universe, an attraction toward the good, the true, and the beautiful.

That tranquility is certainly not a magic recipe for immediately solving all your personal problems, nor is it a solution for the economic crises that are constantly cropping up all over the place and causing much hardship in the world today. However, it is a good antidote for anguish. It has the taste of prophetic serenity about it, which could be contagious.

Its savor is unique. Have confidence, then. Most of all, have confidence in God. Your spiritual roots do exist, and they will bring forth fruit. Trust in God!

Have confidence in yourself. It's not so easy to have faith in your own capabilities, to carry out without regret the choices that direct your life.

Have confidence in others as well, remembering that diversity creates harmony and beauty, and that being different does not mean being hostile. A meadow in the mountains is beautiful when it is magnificently strewn with many different species of flowers.

Don't think too much about a lazy kind of tranquility that would prefer to avoid troubles of the world, though. This confidence of ours will also be a battle to be waged.

If you feel anxiety growing within you, turn toward God. Catch your breath and hope in Him. Here again, don't hesitate to talk about what is burdening you. Let your pain flow out of you, as one lances an abscess in order to drain the infection from it. And if you are really in turmoil, don't hesitate to seek out and receive the healing graces of the Sacrament of Reconciliation

CHAPTER 12

Sadness

You've surely learned that there is sadness, and then there is **sadness**. If the awareness of your imperfections saddens you sometimes, and if you're a little disappointed with yourself, and feeling somewhat bitter, that's not, strictly speaking, a bad thing, from the point of view that it may unleash within you a desire to make spiritual progress. On the other hand, profound sadness, that consists of being disgusted with yourself, of making you despair, of imagining that you are worthless and loathsome; all these are extremely negative feelings. Generally speaking, sadness does more harm than good. Although it's true that it can prompt us to have some qualms of conscience, it most often engenders anguish, feelings of revolt, jealousy, envy and impatience. That's certainly something to consider. Sadness, then, is another evil that we must combat. It attacks the best of us; it encourages those who act generously to despair, and makes them lose all desire to act. It's been said that the devil weeps over the beauty of the world and rejoices over people's sadness.

Sadness can be very serious, making you feel disgusted with yourself, preventing you from having a clear view of reality, and wiping out all your initiative. It's like a terrible Siberian winter, utterly otherworldly frozen desolation, which removes all beauty from the earth, invades all creatures, and destroys anything that lives.

If you are feeling sad, don't hesitate to turn to prayer, and to the Sacrament of Reconciliation and confession. Do your best to fight this movement of spiritual depression that wells up within you. Resist!

It's also a good idea to make a decision to get busy with other things, to make you useful, and to help carry the burdens of others. Don't wallow in self-pity. Seek out the company of cheerful and spiritually mature people who can help you to regain your energy.

CHAPTER 13

Should we wait to feel spiritual consolations before we pray?

The Bible tells us that God's creative action in this world is conducted in perpetual motion. Sometimes, indeed, we have the impression that this motion is cyclical, and that everything is eternally beginning again. Day turns into night, then into day, spring into summer, summer into autumn, autumn into winter and winter into spring again. However, if we are really attentive, we'll see that none of our days resembles the preceding one.

In many parts of the world this is true for the weather; foggy days alternate with sunny ones, the North Wind is broken by a spell of balmy weather. This diversity gives an incredible beauty to our universe. The same is true of you. The Ancients used an extraordinary expression to refer to humanity; they called humans *"the microcosm"*—a universe in microscopic size. I believe this to be true. Each person is like a tiny universe, and in each individual there exists, in microcosm the extraordinary complexity of all of nature.

If you tried to precisely define the infinite variety of the nuances of your impressions, your moods, and your feelings, you would be exhausted. At times you are at the summit of youthful enthusiasm; energetic and resolute, shortly afterward you feel defeated and depressed, invaded by a humid fog of the blues. Between these two extremes there exists within you a whole pallet of feelings. There is never a day, nor even an hour that is exactly like any other.

Under such circumstances it's not easy to stay on an even keel of emotions and to live with total confidence in God and in yourself. And yet, you are invited to witness to that *"prophetic serenity"* of which the Gospel speaks, although so many things turn and change around you.

Whatever happens, I suggest that you remain confident and keep your eyes fixed on God. Yes, eyes fixed on God! I imagine you as being a bit like one of those great sailing ships that courageously goes forth to breach the waves. Whether your boat sails facing into the wind or with it to your back, heading east or west, no matter what the force of the wind, the needle of your compass always points to the North. And if the seas are stormy and even if your boat is in danger of capsizing, not just on rough outer seas, but within yourself because of your problems with navigating, keep your eyes fixed on God. As your days go by, you will be sad or joyful; in the dark night of storm or in the full light of day; feeling the refreshing sprays of the sea or weathering icy squalls. The point of the inner compass of your spiritual life will always be fixed on the star that is the Love of your Creator. *"Nothing can separate us from the love of*

God," St. Paul reminds us, who himself stood firm while withstanding a record number of blows for his faith in Christ.

Would you like to make a resolution to always maintain your interior compass? I'm told that when the wind is very strong, bees take hold of tiny stones in order to ballast their little bodies in flight and return safely to their hives. I don't know whether this is true, but it's such a lovely image, and one that corresponds so perfectly with what I'm trying to say! That resolution to maintain your compass will give you a good interior *"ballast."* It will not keep you from confronting a storm, but it will allow you to face it courageously.

That said, here are four more points on this subject which I'll allow myself to present to you in somewhat of an outline:

1. You've noticed that the spiritual life doesn't consist in gathering moments of intense happiness; that you will not weep every night with tenderness and joy; that you will not always wear an angelic smile, making you a being set apart from others. I have not given you any false advertising.

   In order to better explain my thinking, I'd like to bring up another episode from the bible. I don't expect it to astonish you at all. In the story of David, there is an extraordinary event. David was still a very young man when King Saul decided, in his paranoid delirium, to assassinate him. The king placed himself at the head of his elite company of commandoes. Hour by hour the perimeter of his operations of pursuit tightened dangerously around the mountainous area where the fugitive David had taken refuge with a few companions. Having arrived near some caves, King Saul entered one in order to take care of his personal needs. But he had chosen the exact one where David and his companions were hidden. We have to believe that going from the bright light of day into the dark obscurity of the cave temporarily blinded the king. But the young outlaws were armed, and could very well have taken advantage of that moment when their enemy was otherwise occupied. David made a sign to the other hideaways to allow the king to leave. It was only when Saul was just outside the opening of the cave that David burst out, brandishing in his hand a piece of the royal mantle, which he had succeeded in cutting off without being seen by the king.

This is a great story that perfectly illustrates the personal qualities of young David. But it's the end of the story that really interests me now. King Saul was completely overcome. A great fear had taken hold of him when he realized the danger he had been in, as well as a great admiration for this wonderful young man who had spared him. He began to sob, and to publicly regret his conduct. He called David *"my son,"* and prophesized that he would become a great king. However, nothing is ever quite so simple, not even in the Bible. In spite of that picturesque and happy event, Saul did not change, and shortly afterward his delirium and his persecutions of David began once again.

There are some people who, like King Saul, suddenly become very moved by the Goodness of God and seem to be quite overcome by their religious experience, to the point where we could say without any doubt that their hearts are expanding with love of Him. But these dispositions are like summer showers. They don't last, and produce only the mushrooms of superficial impressions. Those involved quickly return to their old bad habits.

This attitude resembles that of a little child whom I observed in the following situation. His mother who was suffering from an abscess had gone to the health clinic in her neighborhood, bringing the child with her. Seeing the doctor made an incision in his mothers abscess, the child became dissolved in tears. If he'd been strong enough, he would even have fought the surgeon, who seemed to him to be forcing his mother to suffer. However, hardly had they left the clinic, when the child began to eat some chocolate that he had in his pocket. When his mother asked him for a little piece, the child threw a tantrum, categorically refusing to share any of it with his mother for whom he shed so many tears just a short time before.

Sometimes we are overcome by the message of the Gospel, feeling ourselves intellectually and emotionally very close to this wounded God who suffers for humanity. However as soon as we return to the reality of our daily lives, it happens that we feel ourselves to be incapable of carrying through with our good resolutions. To be a Christian does not just consist of feeling emotionally moved by the Gospel and having our hearts touched by the person of Christ. No! To serve God is to Seek Him in our neighbor and to act very concretely, putting us at the service of others.

2. That said, it is sometimes extremely agreeable to feel a very strong love for the Word of God, and to have intense spiritual experiences. It motivates us to pursue the spiritual life. The Bible tells us in Psalm 118:103 that the Word of God is *"....sweeter than honey to my mouth."*

   It seems that in a faraway country an herb exists that takes away all hunger and thirst. It allows the nomads who roam the deserts to prolong their journeys and to overcome their fatigue. We sometimes have these fore-tastes of what we will later find in that state of eternal transfiguration to which we are called by the Resurrection. Alexander the Great discovered something similar in the beautiful scents of *"Happy Arabia."* This gave his companions the courage to investigate those neighboring lands. The strong spiritual feelings that we can feel in our prayer and the satisfaction that we draw from our interior lives are encouragements from which we can surely profit. However, we mustn't use these criteria for the success and efficacy of our relationship with God.

3. It can also happen that the positive feelings we have in prayer come from ourselves. This is our narcissistic side that delights in what we think to be prayers. So how can you distinguish if God is acting, or if you are just

pleasing yourself in those moments that you are actually giving to yourself rather than to God? How can you know if your prayer is valid and successful?

The best way to know the quality of your prayer is by the fruits it will give you, not by the satisfactions and feelings that it produces in you. If, after your prayer you know how to be more generous, more attentive to others, if you are more willing to serve others, you will then have good reason to believe that your prayer is good and that it is bringing you into true relationship with your God. If, on the other hand, while feeling extraordinary times of union with your God, while feeling extreme happiness in praying to Him, you are aggressive, abrupt, surly as soon as you leave your prayer, believe me, you still have nothing of the saint about you. A good tree only produces good fruits, the Gospel of Matthew tells us in Chapter 7.

4. If you have strong, happy spiritual feelings in your prayer, remain humble, and don't attribute that experience to your extraordinary capacity to pray magnificently. The person who eats candy can't say that his mouth is sweet, but rather the candy. If God sends you strong feelings in prayer, it's a free gift from Him. Realize that you are still like the little children who need sugar in their milk. In the beginning, God showers you with sweets in order to encourage you. Take advantage of everything He gives you in prayer. Ask yourself this question, *"Why does God give me these special moments?"* Undoubtedly, it's in order to strengthen my relationship

with Him, and especially to encourage me to become better in my relationships with my neighbor. If He has allowed you to discover extraordinary energy in your prayer, it's so that you can become even more involved in the service of others.

Pray also in the times when it's not so appealing to you. Certain times will be marked by a total absence of that feeling of intense satisfaction that pleased you so much. Be ready to live all of the seasons of your relationship to God interiorly; the joyful times of easy prayer and the wintry times in which no inspiration comes to you, the fogs of discouragement, and the springs of renewed desire. It's also a good idea to make a decision to get busy with other things, to make yourself useful, and to help carry the burdens of others. As I've said so many times before, don't wallow in self-pity. Seek out the company of cheerful and spiritually mature people who can help you to regain your energy.

CHAPTER 14

When your morale is low

If you have had the pleasure of receiving great spiritual consolations, you will know that this *"springtime"* does not last forever. In your prayer, as in your work in the service of others, you will have certain times of *"dryness,"* where you will feel like you are traveling through a spiritual desert.

What should you do during these times? First, reflect clearly. Look to see where this impression of dryness is coming from. It may be that it simply comes from within yourself. There could be other reasons for it, though, which I'd like to propose to you in the following six points:

1. God may wish to withdraw the sugar from your feelings during your prayer, like a mother tries not to make her baby's bottle too sweet. This could, however, be just a guess on your part, because God's intentions are often quite difficult for us to figure out.

2. Maybe you are not too fervent in your prayer, and you do it as a kind of chore; something that has to be done *"in spite of everything."*

3. You may be lying on a bed of good feelings and self-satisfaction while God is knocking at your door, without you hearing Him. Then you are like the young lady in the Song of Songs in the Bible. Taking a risk, the young man who loves her comes at night and knocks on her windowpane. But the young lady is in bed; she doesn't want to get up. Being in a bad mood and half asleep, she orders him to leave and let her sleep in peace. Then, a little later, in a flash of insight, she realizes that she has just missed a wonderful encounter with her beloved. She bounds out of bed and runs into the night to find him, but it's too late for this meeting...if this young lady is sad, it's her own fault after all!

4. You are not being honest with yourself or with your spiritual director, which puts a false face on your description of your spiritual life.

5. All of your attention is on the things you have to do in your life. It's impossible, then for you to take the time or to be in the frame of mind necessary to be available for a true encounter with God.

6. You are expecting to find exactly the same strong feelings you had during certain moments when you first began to pray. As a result, you are feeling very disappointed.

All these things can contribute to drying up your joy in praying. Find out which one may be affecting you, but don't spend too much time in self-analysis. Be honest with yourself. If you can diagnose rather quickly what the problem is that is preventing you from pursuing your spiritual life happily, just the fact of locating and identifying the problem can already be the beginning of the solution.

Having completed this inspection, I advise you to return to your spiritual road in the following ways:

1. Turn back to God, admitting your weakness.
2. Ask the Lord that you may find joy again, using Psalm 1:14; *"Give back the joy of being saved."*
3. Re-center your thinking with the help of your spiritual director.
4. Don't lose heart; remind yourself that you will find happiness once again in your encounter with your God.
5. Don't stop your prayer times for anything!

When it's really nice outside, the bees make more honey and fewer larvae, because the weather is so good that they are extremely busy, and they don't think so much about enlarging their colonies. On the other hand, when the weather is gloomy, foggy, or rainy, they are very busy repopulating their hives. When the spiritual life is easy, and your relationship with God is flooded with the honey of sweet joy in your encounters with Him, outside commitments may be less frequent. However, if that euphoric feeling dissipates, it's a good idea to increase your activities and multiply your opportunities for service to others.

It's a very false idea to think that what we do without any real taste for, is bad. It's true that we would rather offer someone fresh roses so they may enjoy their beauty and scent. But I would like to stress that other actions that are undertaken with less pleasure are just as profitable, dignified and important as any others. They often have more vigor and life; being nourished more by your will than by pleasure alone.

It's not very hard to participate in scouting in the summer when the weather is beautiful. But confronting a rigorous climate and big difficulties for several days in a row will really develop character in young people. Being a rescuer as long as there aren't any accidents where you have to mess up the nice clothing you are wearing is hardly challenging, but being called in to help in an emergency when there has been a natural disaster—now that's something much more difficult that demands qualities of real courage and efficiency.

The same is true of prayer. Prayer that we do out of desire is good, but the one we do when we have to push ourselves a little, even forcing ourselves in the beginning, has a very different savor. Commitments we take on for the pleasure of them are excellent, but action taken because we need to keep our commitments, even if it's difficult, often has a very different efficacy and deeper value.

Always choose what is harder and do it well. This will give you great energy and a holy character. Little by little, you'll see that this battle toughens and strengthens you. Later in life, your choices will depend on these many days when you give your self totally, with all your heart and soul, when you always chose the steeper path.

CHAPTER 15

An example to end this section

I can't resist the desire to end this section by sharing with you a passage from the life story of St. Bernard that I discovered one day while doing some reading.

First, though, I'd like to remind you that my example will illustrate a common phenomenon in almost all those who begin to put themselves at the service of God. In the beginning, things look very promising, and there is much enthusiasm. Then one feels a certain discouragement coming over him in the form of spiritual dryness, which one hadn't expected.

I remember the screams coming from some little scouts when, all of a sudden, the flashlight that lit their way back to camp grew dimmer and dimmer and finally went out. They were terrified of the dark, out of breath, afraid, and so happy to finally find their leaders again.

Reasonable people maintain that no one can remain motivated with out receiving any sort of satisfaction in his or her work. Our personal development depends on gathering positive experiences from our successes and the gratification of our desires. For someone who has invested his or her time and energy in their encounters with God, the feeling of the absence of God suddenly becomes unbearable and completely discourages that person from following that road. I've noticed the same thing with babies who are being weaned from their bottles; they cry their hearts out, trying to find their beloved bottles again, and they make life very hard on their parents.

Let me come back to the story I promised to share with you. The hero is a monk named Geoffrey de Pedronne, a companion of St. Bernard of Clairvaux. This brave young man had just taken his vows, consecrating his whole life to God under the white habit of the Cistercian Order. Suddenly, he felt no more desire for prayer, a complete lack of motivation and a terrible sadness. Can you imagine that? A monk who begins to have no interest in his encounters with God, when everyone knows that these men pray nearly eight hours a day! He starts to find the time going by very slowly. He starts to crumble, nostalgically remembering his buddies, all of them young knights who must be having a wonderful life. He misses his parents too, and the great life of a young squire that he had just renounced. In those days, let me remind you, there was no possibility for a religious person who had taken his vows to go back on his word and leave the monastery!

Although monks speak very little among themselves, one of his brother monks finally noticed his depression. He found a way to approach Geoffrey to question him about it.

"What's happened, Geoffrey? Usually you are happy, smiling, full of enthusiasm, and now you seem completely

deflated!" He sees that this young companion starts to sigh, tears fill his eyes, and he's about to cry.

"*I'll never be happy again. I've made a terrible mistake enclosing myself in this monastery; it's no good...*"

The monk doesn't let the subject drop. The dilemma of his young brother monk has moved him deeply, so he decides to take an unusual step and shares everything with his Father Abbot, who is none other than the famous Bernard of Clairvaux. The Abbot takes him seriously, and offers his prayers right then and there for the intentions of the young monk. At the same time, Goeffey who was completely depressed, had gone to take a nap in order to get a little rest. After a while, both arise, one from the spot where he had succeeded in sleeping, and the other from his conversation with God. But the young monk is now completely transformed; he is so radiant that his companion can't believe his eyes and is very disturbed telling himself that he has bothered his Father Abbot for nothing. But Geoffrey bursts out laughing and tells him:

"*I was telling you the truth when I thought a short time ago that I would never be happy again, but now, I am just as certain of something else; I will never be sad again!*"

I'm going to use this story to form a little outline of the progression that I've often observed in many people whom I've had occasion to accompany in their spiritual lives.

1. At the beginning of a deep relationship with God, we start off by feeling great happiness. In my opinion, it's a

kind of encouragement from God. The Christian road seems luminous and wonderfully enriching.

2. Suddenly, *"the milk and honey"* disappear. This is a very mysterious thing. One is in some way cut off from the mother's milk of his blessings. It's hard. But in order to digest more solid food, the baby must make the sacrifice of his bottle!

3. The resulting crisis can be profound, even terrible. Strong temptations come to assail you. You feel like abandoning the whole idea.

4. This is when you need to stay strong and not give up. Certainly you should never say, like our good brother Geoffrey, *"I will never be happy again,"* because even in the darkest night we know that the dawn will come. Similarly, when you're feeling joyful as a result of having communed well with God in prayer, you should not then say, *"I'll never again have difficulties in my prayer."* No! For, as the wise man says, *"In the days of unhappiness, you must remember the joys of the happy days."* When all is going well, remember that more difficult times are bound to come, and in times of trial, remember the dawn, which will eventually break through the darkness.

5. Above all, don't forget that it's a wonderful and very useful thing to be able to confide in a friend or spiritual director. This allows you to put things in their proper perspective.

I'd also like to add that with certain people, discouragement could come as a result of being overly zealous. They overdo the fasts, sacrifices, and night vigils of prayer. As a result, they are exhausted, haggard, and incapable of being available when they are needed. The body and the spirit are inseparably linked. Don't neglect your body—on the contrary! Weakening yourself by fasting is not a good way of making yourself available to your God and to those who are counting on you. Leave that for a particular form of religious life. St Francis of Assisi himself had to require that his religious not overdo it in their great enthusiasm to inflict penances on themselves. Francis himself endured a long period of depression, which lasted two full years. He no longer had enthusiasm for anything; he who was known by his brothers as always being so full of joy and vitality. After that tempest passed, Francis recovered his radiant, dynamic personality. As a result, don't be surprised if you sometimes go through more austere and difficult periods in your spiritual life too.

PART FIVE

*Making sure you're
on the right road*

CHAPTER 1

A few more thoughts before the end of this work

First of all, I'd like to convince you of how important it is for you to regularly set aside time in your schedule for a personal encounter with your God. By watching *little birds* beat their wings, surely you have noticed that the moment they cease to do so, they rapidly plummet to the ground. Now you may not yet fly yet like an eagle that can soar majestically and nearly effortlessly through the sky of your spiritual life. Instead, like the *little bird*, if you don't maintain the dynamics of your Christian commitments, you won't continue them for very long...and the problem with spiritual plummets is that sometimes they cause us to fall lower than the at moment of our first flight.

The best watches in the world need to be maintained and regulated. Be your own watchmaker in caring for the workings of your spiritual life. I've been very impressed to see how often and with what precision the master watchmaker oils the minute mechanisms that make the watches work. Do the same for yourself. Don't allow yourself to rust! Don't let the wear and tear of daily habits conquer you. Actually, we always need to do battle against the erosion of time. The early Christians were very fond of celebrating anniversaries; these celebrations reinvigorated their faith, and gave them the opportunity to *"reframe"* their spiritual lives. For example, on the feast of the Baptism of the Lord, they began the custom of collectively making a profession of faith.

I'll leave it up to you to choose the best time and place to make a retreat, while following the advice of your spiritual director. To conduct this retreat, I'd like to suggest to you some new colloquies or conversations with God based on the following subjects.

CHAPTER 2

Reflect upon this wonderful truth: God needs you!

1. You've made some good progress, since you first opened this book. You've made the decision to reject a certain amount of temptation that you perceive to be negative. You have found the desire to serve God and your neighbor. When you realize that you've started down the wrong road, now you change course. Are you happy to have accepted this itinerary? Does this road make you joyful?

2. The commitment you've made is to God Himself. If your personal pride would demand that you keep a commitment to a friend, how much more so when you've given your word to your Creator!

3. You're not alone in this commitment. You are entering into the dynamics of the Gospel road, wherein so many witnesses before us have participated. They are with us spiritually on this road.

4. When you made your commitments, God did not *"trap"* you. He captained your ship, not with threats and violence, but in discovering for you the road to happiness.

God is with you as you sail on. God is present with and to you—just as present as he was to the apostles on the day of that frightening storm on the Lake of Galilee.

5. This is a chance for you to discover a road that many others did not find until they neared the end of their lives. Saint Augustine, who had his conversion at age thirty, cried, *"Late have I loved Thee, oh Beauty ever ancient, ever new; late have I loved Thee."* Yes, I repeat, *"it is truly a great blessing to put your youth at the service of your God."*

6. Have you noticed certain changes within yourself? Do you find that you have better self-control? Have you experienced the wonderful energy one can draw from prayer?

After having considered what you've discovered, and what has encouraged you to advance along this road, don't be afraid to thank God and to tell God again of your great trust in Him.

CHAPTER 3

Here is a new outline for spiritual holiness

Now, I'd like to propose a series of themes for reflection which will demand a little more of your time. It's not necessary to go through them all in one sitting. On the contrary, you can go through them a little at a time. It's also not necessary to do these reflections at night, on your knees, a candle in your hand, listening to Gregorian chant on your media device while pretending you are in a dark Roman crypt. You can easily think about them while walking around, or at night while in bed before going to sleep. All I ask is that you try to be attentive to the themes that I suggest to you. Be a little concentrated and try not to spread out your thoughts to cover too many years, though; they'll lose their effectiveness. Don't hesitate to take the time to write down your reflections regarding what you discover in the process.

So, without stopping all your activities and closing yourself up in a monastery, I would suggest that you find a way to have some silent time. It's important to make time for silence so you will not run the risk of being interrupted by the phone, texting, or friends dropping in for a visit. In the hours prior to your reflection time you are not forbidden to think about God; quite the contrary. Thinking about God in the midst of your activities can only help to set the stage for your deeper encounter with Him.

So, as usual, in order to begin well:

1. I invite you to put yourself in the Presence of God.
2. Ask the Holy Spirit to accompany you in your prayer.
3. Offer the Lord your desire to make progress on this road that He is opening to you.
4. If you notice that you did not make as much progress as you expected, don't be at all discouraged. On the contrary, just renew that desire to turn more toward this God who is waiting for you and counting on you.
5. Choose one of the following themes (in these next chapters 4, 5, 6, or 7).

CHAPTER 4

What is my relationship with God?

1. How do I make sure I don't drift away from God? How do I reinforce my spiritual roots while cultivating strong ties with God?

2. How do I feel regarding what God asks of me in His Gospel? Do I feel happy? Do I feel like my life is fulfilled?

3. How do I feel about my minor imperfections? I certainly can't help showing some defects, but do I have any particular concern regarding some aspect of my personality that I am having trouble overcoming? Are there still some temptations contrary to the Gospel that I find attractive, and where I still find some pleasure?

4. Do I enjoy my times of encounter with God? Do I sometimes feel irritated or annoyed by these encounters, or do I sometimes even feel distaste for them? Among the ones that we have spoken of here, what form of prayer has brought you the most satisfaction?
   - Hearing the Word of God
   - reading it
   - discussing it with others
   - meditating

- giving your prayer a more contemplative aspect
- receiving the Sacrament of Reconciliation
- meeting with your spiritual director
- Eucharistic Adoration
- overcoming your whims and desires

What have I found to be difficult or burdensome? Why, in my opinion, are some of these points difficult for me?

5. Am I comfortable with the idea that I love God? Do I think of God during the day? Does it make me happy when I think of God?

In Psalm 86, King David says, *"Gladden the soul of your servant; for to You, O Lord, I lift up my soul."* Is this an idea that is familiar to you? Is this a comfort for you; is it a pleasure to think of the love God has for you? Do you find that you are able to make a short prayer to God in the midst of your activities? Do you sometimes feel that God is right there with you? When one of your friends returns from a long trip, as soon as you hear his voice, you probably drop what you are doing, and think only of being with him again. This sometimes happens with God, that we have a sudden strong feeling; an awareness of His presence, that makes us forget all else for a few seconds.

6. Am I comfortable with the idea that my God came to share the path of men and mine?

7. Do I ever think about all those witnesses who have gone before us in Faith? Do I think that everything that they

went through is a great treasure from which I can profit?

8. How do I speak of God? Do I try to talk about God when the occasion presents itself? Do I like to participate in community prayers where I can use my talents for singing, playing a musical instrument, or reading?

9. In order to concretize my choice of putting the Gospel into practice, have I made a commitment to something where others can profit from my virtues and talents?

10. Have I noticed that I have given up certain habits or made concrete choices for God? Sometime a young man who's in love with a young woman will give up an activity that he really likes in order to prove his love for his beloved. For example, he might give up motorcycle competitions that used to be his main activity on the weekend, because his fiancée is too nervous about it, and he wants to please her. He does it out of love for her, and for their mutual happiness, not out of masochism. In this same spirit, what have I sacrificed for God in my life?

CHAPTER 5

How do I feel about myself?

1. Do I find that I have good self-esteem? Is my opinion of myself perhaps a bit too flattering? Or, on the other hand, do I find that I tend to *"put myself down?"* Do I believe that things other than money might also make good investments: in particular, regarding the spiritual life?

2. What kind of appreciation do I have for my talents and good qualities?

3. In what direction is my heart leaning? Do I have certain passions that don't allow me to make progress in the area of the Gospel?

4. What do I believe to be my worth in the eyes of God? Is the idea that I am loved by God familiar to me? Do I feel very small before Him? It's true that it's not difficult for a fly to feel really minute compared to Mt. Washington, or a drop of water in comparison to the ocean...however; humility doesn't consist of our feeling miserable, but in being aware of what we truly are before God.

5. Am I sometimes apt to overestimate my importance?

6. Am I aware of having adopted any behaviors that are contrary to my good health? I mean, for example, by overeating, not getting enough sleep, overworking, using dangerous stimulants, or taking undue risks?

CHAPTER 6

How are my relationships with others?

1. Do I like other people? My family? My colleagues at work? How are my relationships with my neighbor? Am I kind? Critical or demanding?

   In order to reflect clearly on this point, think about the most difficult and bothersome people you know, those who are really a *"pain in the neck,"* and there are surely some of those in your life! Then, bring to mind those who are unkind to you in their words and actions. What are my true feelings towards them?

2. Do I find that I am really tempted to speak of others in less than flattering terms, and particularly those whom I really dislike? Do I wish evil on certain people? Do I take pleasure in their trials?

CHAPTER 7

What are my passions?

First, take some time to consider your conclusions on the three points that you have just considered; that is, regarding your love of God, of yourself, and of others.

Consider also how you handle your desire to overcome your bad inclinations, your defects, and your sins.

1. Am I realistic with regard to money, pleasure and honors?
2. Do I have confidence in God? Does God play a part in my decision-making?
3. Am I subject to sadness?
4. Can my life be compared to a good stringed instrument; well tuned, one that plays in all the different keys of your desires, your pleasures, and your feelings?

CHAPTER 8

Going a bit further

Once you've been able to explore areas I've proposed to you, in addition I suggest the following themes for your prayer:

1. Thank God for the changes you've noticed within yourself. Be happy to feel God's Presence in your life.
2. In case you should feel that you haven't made much progress, consider how you can remedy that situation by applying more regularity and determination to your exercises.
3. Thank God for His help in keeping your commitments.
4. Ask God's pardon for your infidelities.
5. Ask your creator to give you more generosity.
6. Ask those great witnesses who have gone before us to help you in your prayer and in your commitments.

CHAPTER 9

Taking stock

After having decided where you now stand, if possible with the help of your spiritual director, I propose that you reconsider, during the course of the upcoming days, the themes of the following reflections, according to the same ideas and principles you used in the first part.

CHAPTER 10

Your spiritual resources

You are very lucky to have been able to become aware of the spiritual dimension of your existence. Now you know that you are *"on the road to eternity."* You have understood this wonderful goal, for which your God asks your freedom. You have understood that your liberty can be realized by adhering to it.

Consider with how much generosity you respond to this call from God. St. Augustine, at the end of his extraordinary journey towards the Faith, cried out, *"You have made us for Yourself, O Lord, and our hearts are restless until they rest in You."*

Perhaps when you think about those things that might have formerly disturbed you, or about those things which occupied your time not too long ago, you can better judge the road on which you are now traveling.

Our world is really wonderful in so many ways; the beauty of the mountains, the joy of participating in sports, a smile, a joke, an unforgettable moment; these are all things which beautifully contribute to our attempt at happiness. Yes, our world is wonderful, but all that is only a pale reflection, a sort of imperfect anticipation of the joy that will be ours in knowing God. This universe, limited as it may be, gives us a great lesson. But the loveliest of orchids is born and then returns to dust. The most beautiful sunsets, the sweetest nights of summer, and the most wonderful moments of our existence will still leave us somewhat unsatisfied; sometimes in a way which will even astonish us. That's because we are called to something even greater.

The search for our God puts us on the road toward the infinite, to which we all instinctively aspire. You are made for God. Only by meeting Him will you find that wonderful place which is reserved for you alone, that of an eternal creature. The Promised Land, toward which you are traveling, will fulfill your greatest desires, and will one day make you worthy of infinity.

CHAPTER 11

Be strong in your choices

Many television series often present stories of vengeance in which a wide variety of developments take place. In the space of an hour, and between commercials, the hero, a victim of some sort of aggression, will have the satisfaction of making the perpetrator pay the consequences of his actions. Forgiveness is an outlandish concept, and reconciliation seems to be a very naive and unrealistic idea. However, whenever the news network reports a beautiful example of generosity, people react in an extremely positive manner. There is far more happiness in the latter than in the pale satisfaction of revenge. Having recourse to violence always leaves a bitter after-taste, especially when those consequences are lived out in real-life situations.

Following the Gospel is not just a virtuous idea or the expectation of some future recompense. It's the acceptance of the logic of happiness, which can bring durable solutions to many a dramatic situation.

Upon meeting Christ during the course of her chaotic and unsatisfying personal history, the Woman at the Well asked the Lord, *"Give me to drink."* Ask this of your

God. The water of your Christian commitment does not come forth from some stagnant cistern, but from the actual source of happiness, with which your God desires to fully quench your thirst.

CHAPTER 12

We are in need of saints

Think about the incredible variety of believers who have gone before you over the course of the last twenty centuries. The first ones were often martyrs, as were many others who came after them. Often this consummate witness was given at an extremely young age. Yes, at twelve, thirteen, fifteen, twenty or twenty five years old, they went to the very end of the logic of their choice for God. They suffered all manner of moral and physical tortures for the faith. Some died explicitly for their religious beliefs; others were murdered for the sake of justice, because they were witnesses to the truth, or for hiding fugitives. The causes for which these martyrs died are perhaps those for which we are no longer prepared to die. These martyrs were often young women, who showed just as much courage and daring as the most courageous of young men.

Consider also those who dedicated all of the resources of their brilliant intelligence to explaining and putting into practice the Christian message. Often their courageous positions were not appreciated; they did not always follow the beaten path in demonstrating to others the exigencies of the magnificent road of the faith.

The saints of the Twenty-first Century are among us. The great witnesses of the past have been where we now are. They believed in the same God we do, they thirsted just as much for happiness and truth as we do. They had their own particular talents, just as we do. Yesterday's saints were shepherds or queens, saintly knights or founders of charitable or religious orders. Today they are businessmen, or salesmen, doctors without boarders, pilots, students, athletes and homemakers. Our Church needs saints of today. They won't be people from outer space; it will be you, quite simply, and those who interact, work and recreate with you.

CHAPTER 13

You will be carried

The Cross-on which the Savior died was a brutal invention imported by the Romans, and originally intended to punish rebellious slaves. The crucified person slowly died of asphyxiation, owing to the fearful effort imposed on his body to sustain its own weight, as he battled against its downward pull.

This atrocious physical suffering of Christ on the Cross had been preceded by that wretched night in the Garden of Olives, in that atmosphere of betrayal and cowardice, of abandonment and derision. Our Lord took upon Himself the suffering of all peoples. He confronted evil head-on; so that its absurdity would not be a cause for despair for you.

In a certain manner, you were already present in those final moments of the life of Our Savior. It was for each member of the immense family of humanity that He underwent His Passion, yes, for you, too!

The mother-to-be, while she waited to give birth tenderly prepared all little things that would one day be needed for her child. Christ prepared for your happiness in

His suffering on the Cross that opened and began on the morning of the Resurrection.

Never forget these essential elements of our Faith. *"Christ loved you, and gave Himself up for you,"* St. Paul reminds us. What will be your own response to a gift so absolute!

CHAPTER 14

Yes, you are infinitely loved

Do you know when it was that God actually began to love you? I've often asked myself this question. Here's the answer, which finally came to me after having consulted the texts of the bible at great length. God began to love you when He began to be God. Really? So God began to be God at a certain moment in time? No, surely not. God has always been God; God has no beginning and no end! In other words, God loved you from all eternity, as he did each human being made in His image.

The Book of Jeremiah, among others, says it wonderfully; *"With age-old love I have loved you; so I have kept my mercy for you."* (Jeremiah 31:3). These words are addressed to you personally. Accept them as such. Yes, God thought of you from the very depths of eternity, even before the first morning dawned on the world. Does this cause you to smile a little? Does it still seem pretentious or illusory to you? No! The Bible assures us how precious each person is in his uniqueness. *"Every person is a sacred story."* Humanity is made in the Image of God. Having understood the immense value of your own existence in the eyes of your Creator, this idea can incite you to carry out your own response *"in action"* by the choices that you make in your life.

CHAPTER 15

Concluding our discussion

So? Are you convinced? Convinced of your personal potential to become a saint, or would you prefer to intone the old refrain, *"It's hard, so hard to be a Christian?"*

Your God has given you spiritual roots. The work which we have just undertaken together has, I think, affirmed them, and confirmed them.

I hope that your search will not be simply intellectual. Following Christ does not mean following an idea, a philosophical theory, or a feeling which warms the heart. It is following a Person, a demanding Friend. And this takes place in terms of concrete commitments.

Don't be afraid to follow this road. Be attentive to the rhythms which you will now be able to hear. Don't let your conversations with God fall by the wayside. You're like a young pilot now who, after laving learned by flying as my copilot, is *"ready to solo"* in the sky of the spiritual life. Keep flying...Don't interrupt this pleasure which you have discovered. Pursue your commitments regarding others, live in forgiveness, and nourish yourself in the extraordinary encounter with your God that is offered to you in the Sacrament of Holy Eucharist. Stop to catch breath from time to time. Bon voyage!

CHAPTER 16

What kind of spiritual shape are you in?

In order to follow the dynamic you've begun, I propose a simple rule to you; that of regularly thinking of God during the course of your day, even if only for a fleeting moment. Be happy to think of God often. Be happy about the new direction you're giving to your existence. Around you, life goes on; the earth turns as usual in its orbit, heedless of Him, or so it would seem. But you have changed. And it's very possible that you can actually contribute to making this world a little better than when you came into it.

This fleeting thought of your God will remain completely interior; it will not present a conflict with your many activities. But you will see that the liquid of your newfound resolution will ultimately penetrate all the different layers of your active life.

CHAPTER 17

There have been two objections that I have sometimes encountered which I'd like to bring up

While reading my little book, some may think that the advice I give will simply drown even the best of intentions. Young people will be convinced that it's just not possible to lead an ordinary life with so many religious exercises to do, and that they would have to concentrate night and day on this burdensome activity of seeking God.

Being intelligent is not forbidden! It's also not a question of spending long hours every day on the meditations I've proposed to you. It's not necessary either, to memorize and be able to apply all the laws of the code of civil law before being allowed to vote! Having said that, we know we have only a certain number of hours in a day. King David took charge of all of the interior and exterior politics of his realm, and multiplied his times of encounter with God in a way I wouldn't even dare to suggest. St. Louis was able to find the time to recite all the prayers of a religious monk during the course of his day.

Heads of companies and doctors find the time to go to Mass every day. If you are serious about setting aside time for prayer each day, God will arrange for you to have exactly enough time to do whatever else it is you must do. Believe me, I am speaking from personal experience. If we believe the story of Joshua, the Lord even stopped the sun for a short time so that the people of God had the time to finish what they needed to do! (Joshua 10:121-13). He may not have to go so far as that.

Some will say that prayer is like surfing; some people are just not gifted at it. This little book would then be reserved for an elite few. It's true that I took for granted that you had at least a minimal amount of motivation for your encounter with God, and it's also true that some people really have enormous difficulty in visualizing themselves praying. However, my experience, after visiting the smallest villages in the mountains of my homeland Haute-Savoie, allowed me to observe many things. I saw many different kinds of people, and some who were extremely simple. But I was amazed to see the depth and significance of their spiritual lives. I have never met anyone who cannot pray in one way or another. If there are any difficulties, it is up to us, the spiritual directors, to help them to find the most adequate means to achieve success in prayer.

CHAPTER 18

I can't help giving three last bits of advice as we end our study together

Go back often to the point which I suggested to you in the very first section. Keep your eyes fixed on the Gospel. It's true that certain ground swells will sometimes cause you to drift a bit; that you will deviate from your route, but still, make sure that you follow the general direction of your goal. Don't be afraid of the comments that your choices may engender. Take the means necessary to be faithful to you encounters with your God.

Doctors put a plaque on their doors, and many people are delighted to know they have a doctor as a neighbor, just in case. Don't hesitate to let it be known that you are following a spiritual road, so that others may appreciate your choice in this vein. Do this, not to make yourself appear better than others...that would be a grave mistake. Instead, let it be to witness to the joy you have found along this road. There are many people who will be happy to share this good news which you have discovered.

Finally, climb the mountain of your existence, keeping your eyes fixed on the summit. You are on a journey, so you will cross certain places that will be only steps along the way. Some landscapes will be wonderfully beautiful; others will make you dizzy and will exhaust you. Don't lose sight of the beauty of your personal journey; it is already the road to eternity.

Give Glory to the Father, the Son, and the Holy Spirit, today and every day of your life, forever and ever.